BRAIN XP

Endorsements

Some people were born to inspire others. Some people have the innate ability to draw people to them, to make people listen, and to make people want to connect. Christine has all of this in spades, and to be as grounded and talented as she has shown in her work, is a blessing. She has a powerful story not only of enduring mental illness, but of overcoming it and ultimately redefining it for her generation. In telling her story, she started the process of creating a community that will impact untold numbers of people in the months and years to come. While I'm excited for the world to read this chronicle of her life's journey so far, I'm even more excited to see where the launch of *Brain XP* takes her from here.

Billy Dorsey
Grammy, Dove & Stellar Award-Winning Music Producer
Gospel Recording Artist & Songwriter
Outreach Pastor, Lakewood Church

It is so rare to hear from someone so young about the struggles of mental health. It is even rarer that someone would embrace her struggles and re-define them into something positive. Christine's vision of Brain XP explores the global issue of mental health through the perspective of someone living it. Whether you're a teenager with your own struggles, a mental health professional, a parent, a teacher, or a friend of someone who can relate to Christine's story, the journey she takes you on through her words gives a unique insight to view mental illness through a new lens. Her vulnerability, passion, positivity, and drive to take action are not only inspirational, but educational.

Ashley Phillips
Occupational Therapist
Poway Unified School District

In this honest and brave memoir, Christine is a champion for adolescents and young adults with mental illness who are in desperate need of hope and support.

Aubrey Good
Program Coordinator
International Bipolar Foundation

Brain XP takes us through the journey of a remarkable young lady as she strives to overcome obstacles that most find difficult to understand. Witnessing her struggles firsthand, I am extremely proud of her resiliency, determination, and continued efforts to educate and offer support for others.

Mr. Jared Izidoro
English & Social Science Teacher, Football Coach
Mater Dei Catholic High School

I first met Christine at a National Alliance for Mental Illness (NAMI) conference in California in 2017. I had been invited to present at a breakout session on the topic of my family's twenty-year struggle with my son's severe mental illness. He was first diagnosed with bipolar disorder in middle school when he was the same age that Christine is now. Christine and her mom stopped by my conference booth where I was selling my book telling the story of my family's journey. Christine, her mom, and I had an immediate connection and quickly shared many common experiences and understandings about mental illness.

The outcome of this meeting was a professional agreement that I would work with Christine to publish her first book, *Brain XP.* The compassion I felt for her and her family was very personal. You cannot read Christine's book without grasping the true meaning of psychosis. It is the most horrible part of mental illness, leading the individual experiencing it to lose oneself in a vortex of unreal experiences that are totally real for that person. Christine is brave, unashamed, and determined to set the record straight on psychosis. With the words and maturity level of a bright, young teenager, she tells it like it is—no fancy medical descriptions of hallucinations and delusions, rather the frightening visions and threatening trickery that she lived with every day. The story is simply told but complex in content. As her editor, I counted twenty-four separate incidents of the impact of psychosis on Christine's daily life including isolation, self-harm, running away, confused reality, and eventually hospitalization.

My last comment is for family members—your teens will likely not tell you what they are experiencing in their brains, because they do not understand it themselves. Reading *Brain XP* will give you information from the next best source, another teenager who has lived this brain disorder and is telling you the honest truth.

Benny Malone, M.S.W.
Mental Health Advocate, Consultant, and Writer
Author of *Psychotic Rage! A True Story of Mental Illness, Murder, and Reconciliation*

BRAIN XP

Living with Mental Illness
A Young Teenager's Perspective

Christine Marie Frey

Foreword by Kristin Cadenhead, M.D.

Spring, Texas

BRAIN XP

Published by Benny Malone,

Mental Health Advocacy and Consulting (MHAC)

1214 Dunston Falls Drive, Spring TX 77379

ISBN: 978-1986069014

Cover Design: Debbie Beavers, Plain Yellow Pumpkin

Interior Design: Benny Malone, Mental Health Advocacy and Consulting (MHAC)

Lyrics: Christine Marie Frey

I dedicate this book to the Brain XP Community.
We are the change this world needs.
We are special,
unique, strong, and
we have the power to make a difference.
Never forget how important you truly are.

Contents

Foreword   13

Acknowledgments   15

Christine XP

Introduction   17

Chapter 1   Get to Know Me   23

Chapter 2   The Mask   29

Chapter 3   Is It Me?   41

Chapter 4   "Beautifull" of Love   49

Chapter 5   "Babygirl"   59

Chapter 6   May 13th   75

Chapter 7   Spare Heart   95

Chapter 8   Shy   107

Chapter 9   Okay   113

Chapter 10   Stop Hiding   123

Three Perspectives

A Glimpse Behind the Mask

My Mom's Perspective   133

A Friend's Perspective   150

My Grandparents' Perspective   152

About the Author

About Christine   156

Christine's Blog   157

Christine's Music   166

Online Resources

Mental Health Resources for Teens   168

Foreword

The term "Brain Expanded," or "Brain XP," perfectly depicts the growth experience of this young author. As she describes her early challenges in overcoming her fears, injuries, and tumultuous moods, the reader can feel her determination, resilience, and growth in the face of adversity from an early age. She turns her own experience of struggling to understand herself into an example for others to learn from and at the same time develops her creative potential through media, poetry, music, writing, and advocacy as a means to cope. Christine's journey demonstrates an incredible resilience and self-awareness that has helped to unleash an amazing talent for helping others through her art. Rather than hide, isolate, and feel embarrassed, she tackles stigma head on. She embraces the challenge to educate and lead by example. What began as a simple YouTube video to explain her diagnosis to friends and family developed into moving poetry, musical performances, collaborations with other artists, her own book at age sixteen, and opportunities to advocate for others across the United States and beyond.

Christine's intimate experience with mental health issues also exemplifies the importance of community outreach and education regarding early identification of mental illness in youth. Early recognition of warning signs by family, friends, teachers, and clergy can assure young people get the help they need and perhaps prevent some of the devastating consequences of emerging mental health issues. With proper diagnosis, treatment, and ongoing support from mental health professionals, family and friends can assure the young person finishes school, thrives socially, and goes on to find his or her passion in life. May we all learn from Christine and her story!

Kristin Cadenhead, M.D.
Professor of Psychiatry
University of California San Diego

Dr. Cadenhead is Director of the Cognitive Assessment and Risk Evaluation (CARE) Program, UCSD; Medical Director of the Mental Health Primary Care Clinic, Veterans Administration Medical Center; Associate Residency Training Director, Department of Psychology, School of Medicine; and Clinical Foundations Director, School of Medicine.

Acknowledgements

Thank you to all my family members, friends, teachers, counselors, and therapists who have supported me throughout my life, especially along my Brain XP journey. You have adapted your lifestyles to help me succeed and your kindness will never be forgotten. I'm so proud that each and every one of you chose to stick by my side through the ups and downs of my illness. You are all beautiful examples of strength. We have all learned that the pain was not only faced by me. Despite stereotypical portrayals of mental illness, you overcame fear to lend an open heart and helping hand to me. You have played a major role in my creation of Brain XP, and you have impacted me in such positive ways. I am so proud to announce through my book, album, and my own actions that we are one step closer to ending the concept of mental illness and making Brain XP the sole term that is used to describe all people facing mental health challenges as well as all their supporters. Please know I could not have made it to the place I am now without you. I love you all, and again, I thank you.

Introduction

What is Brain XP?

True passions can be hard to find. I have been fortunate enough to have developed interests in life that led me to realize my passion when I was thirteen years old. The insight came to me in a single moment of extreme frustration. I was getting ready to walk my dog, Sparky, with my mom. I could not face the fact that I had experienced psychosis and never anticipated that later I would be diagnosed with bipolar disorder. I never shared my real diagnosis with anyone because I was afraid they would look at me differently or treat me unkindly. Well, almost never. I told a girl one time that I had been diagnosed as bipolar. The first thing she did was take a huge step back and start walking away. It was then I realized what "stigma" is. The emotional impact of this memory will always stick with me.

As I tied my shoelaces and put the leash on Sparky, it hit me: *I am not my diagnosis.* I am not going to be labeled. My diagnosis does not define me. I am my own person. As Mom and I started out on our walk with the Sparkman, I spoke my mind. I told my mom that people experiencing mental health issues are not crazy. We are simply different. I said, "We need to think of a better way to talk about mental illness and mental health in general. I am fed up with the stigma, the bullying, and the ignorance!"

I've always believed that I was put on Earth for a reason. I've made massive mistakes and my path in life has not always been clear. Deep inside, though, I've always known I have purpose. That is when Brain XP was born. During our walk, Mom and I brainstormed different ways to talk about people who experience mental health struggles and Brain XP was by far our best idea.

Brain XP stands for Brain Expanded, and that is exactly how I feel mental illness should be described. People who have mental disorders are most often extremely creative and insightful in many ways.

Our brains are expanded. I have seen things and heard things that make it seem like I am crazy. The truth is the rest of the world will never see or hear the things that my brain has allowed me to experience. We are all different, so no one should ever feel ashamed.

Brain XP may sound like a silly term my mom and I created out of annoyance and irritability on a twenty-minute dog walk, but it has come a long way. I would have never imagined that this silly term would give me the hope to move past my difficulties, but it has.

My life is real. I am meant to be here. I know that. I am not telling my story to prove anything to anyone. Advocating is my passion. The only reason I'm sharing my story is in the hope that it might help you.

Want to Know More About the Brain XP Community?

My Brain XP Friends—Brain XP is a community I created which is dedicated to ending the stigma toward other teenagers who have mental challenges such as anxiety, depression, bipolar disorder, and schizophrenia. Each of these brain disorders may include symptoms of psychosis if inadequately treated or left untreated. Psychosis is a serious and ugly set of symptoms that only make your life more confusing, scary, and painful. You will learn more about psychosis as you read about the psychotic symptoms I experienced.

The Brain XP education approach includes using contemporary music, books, videos, social media, and public speaking designed to reach out to teenagers worried about their mental health and to show them they are not crazy nor are they alone. Before each chapter, you will see the song lyrics of my ten songs on the music album that will be released with this book. The lyrics are the cover page to the chapter that was inspired by that particular song. Reading the lyrics first may give you a preview of the chapter and help you understand why I say our brains are unique—EXPANDED (XP).

Why is it helpful to think of the brain of a person struggling with a brain disorder as EXPANDED? Because in our struggle and recovery from the pain, confusion, fear, and loneliness, we learn many difficult life lessons and grow to understand ourselves better. We can take those lessons and empower each other to encourage all struggling teenagers to join us in Brain XP and help bring more education, understanding, and acceptance to the world about the authentic reality of mental illness.

Creating Brain XP has been an incredible experience. The whole process took an immense amount of hard work, but I learned so much that every moment spent was worth it. I created Brain XP to help myself, but more importantly, I created it to help others. I hold a special place in my heart for teenagers struggling with mental health disorders because I am one with you.

Please know that anyone can be a part of the Brain XP Community—NOT just struggling teens. Supporters, family members, friends, teachers, therapists, and people looking for more knowledge on a topic that is often frowned upon can be Brain XP. The list extends to everyone in this world with an open heart and open mind to understand these illnesses and fight the stigma surrounding them. ANYONE can be a part of the Brain XP Community.

Everyone is welcome. Please join me!

Christine XP

Our brains are expanded to:

Think with enhanced creativity.
Reason with increased empathy.
Reflect with superior insight.

—Christine XP

Get to Know Me

stayed up late try'na write this song
but it's you who puts me in the zone
but I don't got a chance
'cuz they say that she's just the crazy girl
you don't even want her in your world
she's worthless (I wish I would just say)

Get to know me
Givin' you a chance to see
that if you get to know me
I'm not the person I'm made out to be

I don't need to defend myself
your words are burning hell
and I can't stop you
if I could I would baby dear
'cuz it's becoming so very clear that
help is something you refuse (I wish I would just say)

I'm Brain XP

Chapter One

Get to Know Me

One of the most important lessons in life I've learned is the true meaning of "luck." Luck is practically nonexistent, and I feel God's well-deserved praise has been overlooked because of the concept of luck. We hear each other say, "Oh you're so lucky!" Not nearly as many people say, "Thank you, God for blessing me." In reality, every single time we "get lucky," we have just been blessed by God. I acknowledge that my life has been blessed greatly. I have great parents, a great brother, a great home, and so much more. I could literally go on forever listing all the amazing things in my life that I am grateful for. Counting my blessings has gotten me through challenging times in life. God gives the hardest battles in life to the people He feels can handle them. He doesn't bless you any less than He blesses me. He doesn't bless you any more than He blesses me. He just knows we are capable of different challenges in life. Your challenges and the way you handle them will define your journey.

The journey God planned for me has developed into an amazing path. It is not an easy path, but it has shaped me into the person I am and the person I will continue to become.

I was born with very good health. My mind was quick to understand things and I was really smart.

I grew up in sunny San Diego, California, and I never moved houses. My parents wanted my brother and me to have stable friendships, so we were fortunate enough to stay in one house and keep many great friends growing up.

I have the kind of family that is extremely interactive with each other. My parents, my brother, and I do everything together.

When I think about my family, the words that immediately come to mind are support and love. Those two things, loving and supporting each other, created our foundation. They have kept our family together despite my illness that created so much stress in our lives. We want to spend time with each other and I do believe that is what helped us form strong bonds. We are by no means perfect but have a sense of happiness in our home. That's really all that matters.

As I grew older, I became a very outgoing person. I loved pre-school and I loved playing with the other children. Because I was a fast learner, elementary school was easy for me. I honestly saw it as an opportunity to spend more time with my friends. My behavior was very good. When the teacher was talking, I was listening. When my friends fooled around during class, I was paying attention. I did as I was told, which is why I think I enjoyed school so much. I was never in trouble, so I had no reason to dislike it.

I flew through the first few grades of school with practically no problems academically. However, there were two not so wonderful issues I remember dealing with in elementary school—my obsession over germs and being clean and my frequent feelings of anxiety. I felt I always had to be clean and that no one could touch my food. I didn't think of this obsession with germs and cleanliness as a big issue at the time. It was just how I was. However, it got progressively worse as I continued to grow older.

I also started to realize that I would get anxious in situations where I didn't have control. I needed to know exactly what was going to happen in every situation or else my anxiety would start to show.

I was actually very good at hiding my anxiety and it worked for a while. I felt I had to hide it because everyone thought I was the ideal student who didn't get in trouble and always got straight "A's." I was not supposed to have problems in life, especially problems that had to do with insecurity. I was naturally a confident person, so I pretended that feelings like anxiety, were not there inside me. I did not want to deal with them, so I didn't.

My Brain XP Friends:
"Get to Know Me," both the song and the chapter, are my welcome to you from Brain XP. I wrote the lyrics during a time in my life when I felt as if nobody understood me. False statements are made so quickly, and this song encourages everyone to get to know others and accept them for who they are rather than judging them by what they see on the surface or what is said about them by others. People are not always who they've been made out to be. This chapter will help you get to know me.

Christine XP

Thoughts?

Check out the Brain XP website for my current blog,
music, videos & performances

www.brainxpproject.com

The Mask

Rip it up
Tear it off
Face is shown out loud
Turn around
Check it out
Hear every single sound
and now
the mask is down

Now I know how hard it feels to fall
How painful it is to cry
How hard it is to force yourself
Not to let your composure die
And how hard it is to be vulnerable
How painful it is to say goodbye
How hard it is to just let go
Without the answers to your whys

Why did things happen like this?
Why could I not handle it?
And why didn't I see the signs?
Why didn't I just quit?
And why did I get a second chance?
It's not like I could fix
Everything that just went bad
I guess I was really worth it

Brace yourself
You won't look the same as before
Is it really me
who's inside that girl?
and now
the mask is down

Chapter Two

The Mask

My fourth-grade year was the last year in my life that I consider a relatively easy one. My issues were still minor. They were so minor that nobody around me even noticed them. At times, they were so minor I didn't even notice them.

I was still the top student who had lots of friends, played sports, and interacted effortlessly. Everything truly seemed fine, but something changed within me between the time I exited fourth grade and entered fifth grade.

Somewhere in that time frame, my anxiety level really started to increase. I was still very good about hiding it. I didn't want any attention drawn to myself. I remember hurting my ankle playing soccer at recess, but I didn't say anything. I just continued to play and kept my head down. Three weeks later when I ran the school's mini-marathon the pain became so unbearable I couldn't walk. I won my class's heat, but went to the doctor and found out my ankle was broken.

I also struggled with myself because I couldn't comfortably hang out at my friends' houses. I needed to feel in control in every situation and unfortunately it was simply not realistic for me to have control in every situation. I was too embarrassed to talk to my friends about the matter. So, I pushed myself to continue hanging out with them, even if it meant I had to struggle through uncomfortable circumstances.

I pushed my limit too far. The anxiety grew; it went from being a problem that I had once reasonably handled to a situation that I could not manage. I could no longer sleep over at any other house except for mine. I had horrible anxiety as nighttime approached when

I was at someone else's house. By the time I was ready for bed, I couldn't sleep. In the pit of my stomach, I felt panic. There was nothing wrong. Nobody had said or done anything that triggered me to want to go back to my house. I simply had no clue what was causing that anxiety, but it became too much for me to handle.

As I entered fifth grade, I felt so low. It was embarrassing when the anxiety kept me from going to sleepovers. I put up an internal mask. I pretended the problem wasn't there. When I went to school, I was still the energetic, bubbly student everyone knew. But it didn't matter how I looked or acted, the problem was still there. The girls in my class planned sleepovers for their birthdays, and I literally had no idea what to do. I found an excuse for every instance when I would have to sleep over somewhere other than my own home. I felt pathetic.

Only one of my friends knew about my difficulties. I had tried going to her house to sleep over three times, and every single one of those times, my mom had to come pick me up during the night to bring me home. I was very grateful to my friend that she kept my difficulties between us, but I still felt stuck.

For months, I kept my mask up. I knew I needed to fix my problem, but I didn't know how. Time continued to pass, and not one solution came to mind. I was terrified because I was getting close to ending fifth grade, and sixth grade was coming.

In sixth grade, there was a big five-day camping trip. My whole class drove to a camp site over an hour away. The plan was to sleep in cabins, hike on trails, and do lots of other activities. It was an educational camping trip.

Just thinking about it, my anxiety levels skyrocketed. I had three worries. I had never been camping before. I could not go on sleepovers away from home. Finally, the camping trip was not optional, and a lot of school work surrounded it.

Fifth grade ended, and sixth grade approached so incredibly quickly. As my summer ended and sixth grade started, my stress level doubled in anticipation of the new school year. No improvements or changes had taken place during the three summer months. I knew everything would be the same, but worse.

My mom sat down with me a few days before sixth grade officially started. She told me I needed counseling. My immediate reaction was completely negative. I was shocked. I didn't think I needed therapy. I honestly couldn't even understand why my mom would bring that up. I felt angry that we were even at the point of discussing it at all.

Then reality literally smacked me in the face. My problems were not getting better. They were getting worse. If I didn't do something about them, I would face the humiliation of not being able to go to sixth-grade camp. Not going would harm my grades immensely. Sixth-grade camp was six months away and I needed help. Thankfully, I could acknowledge that.

I was not happy, but I agreed to go to therapy. I started going to see my therapist right when the school year started. I would go once a week to talk to him.

He was really nice. I had a valuable experience working with him, but I still felt incredibly insecure. I still felt embarrassed talking about my inability to sleep during sleepovers. He was patient with me. We worked every week to reframe the negative outlook I had on sleepovers. My eyes were opened to a new sense of positivity.

We moved very slowly, but he saw progress. To be completely honest, I didn't see the improvements he saw. I had been going to therapy for four months. Sixth-grade camp was only two months away. I needed a much bigger sense of confidence to feel prepared for the trip. And to add another factor into my anxiety, I had just broken my same ankle a second time during soccer practice.

31

It was then my therapist and I decided to do a test run. I needed to pick a place to sleep over, and I needed to do my very best at making it through the night. It would just be a trial, so I didn't have too much to worry about. I just needed to be able to spend the night away from home. I felt so scared just thinking about camp. I needed to succeed. I needed something positive to hold on to. I needed to have a good experience. I needed this trial to be amazing.

I decided to choose my grandparents' house as the place to sleep over. On the day of the sleepover trial, I honestly felt scared. I was so nervous to even try. This was the first time in my life that I truly felt alone.

My brother was sleeping over at my grandparents' house with me, and that really was a big relief for me. Having someone else there was such comfort, even though he might not have known that. My parents and grandparents might not have known that. I knew it, though, and I knew I'd have someone to help me in case things went wrong. When I knew my anxiety would be taking over, I always had to have some sort of backup plan. I planned for the worst. But I felt I could make it through with my brother as backup.

My brother and I went with my grandparents on a Saturday evening. They took us to get roast beef sandwiches for dinner. Everything was fine. Everything was good. Everything seemed to be going great.

We got back to their house and watched TV for a while. My mind was everywhere which is probably why I can't remember what shows we watched.

It was starting to get dark outside and I could feel the mask coming over me. I needed a way to hide my fear. I needed to succeed, which made me think I needed to hide all my emotions. It wasn't until my grandparents went upstairs to go to sleep that I began to panic. My anxiety was climbing within me. I had already gotten into my pajamas. I had already brushed my teeth. I was completely ready for bed. I just didn't know how to fall asleep. It was easy at home. I could fall asleep there, no problem. But now I was in a different place, and I simply could not sleep. My thoughts ran too fast and too deep.

My brother and I had the whole living room for the night. He slept on one couch, and the second couch was for me. The hallway bathroom light was left on in case either of us needed to use the bathroom. The TV was on in case we wanted to watch something as well.

When I saw my brother start to fall asleep, I felt even more alone. I was stuck, and I didn't know what to do. My anxiety was building. My heart was racing, and I couldn't help but feel pathetic that this was all over a stupid sleepover.

I tried to wake up my brother to see if he wanted to watch TV with me, but he was already so asleep that he didn't wake up. I went back to my couch and tried to fall sleep. Instead, I kept looking at the clock to see if any time had passed. Of course, time passes slowly when you're staring at the clock every minute.

I got up again and walked to the bathroom. I stared in the mirror and was surprised. I saw an eleven-year-old girl with such fear and sadness in her eyes. I could not believe that little girl was me.

I continued to stare until I finally backed away from the mirror. I looked up, and I started talking to God. It was silent, but He was supposed to always be there. I had Him. Everybody else may have been asleep, but God was with me. I knew it.

I asked for His help. I wanted to get through the sleepover so badly, but I physically and mentally didn't know how.

I finished my conversation with God and tiptoed back to my couch. My brother was still asleep, but I knew everything would be okay. It would not be an easy night, but I would make it through. It was midnight when I went back to the couch, and I continued to struggle to fall asleep. I laid there for a while and then checked the clock. Time was moving, but it was still slow. I laid on the couch for the rest of the night following the same pattern. Try to fall asleep then check the clock. I did that over and over again until it was morning. It felt like I never slept at all, but I probably fell asleep in patches throughout the hours of the early morning.

I was so happy to have followed through. It was rough, but at least I knew I was capable of sleeping over. I was actually a little shocked I got through it. My confidence was building, and my self-esteem was rising. The feeling of relief overwhelmed me. It was a success. God had been my backup plan.

A few weeks later, I had my final test run at my friend's house and again, it was a success. I felt confident there was nothing separating me from having a great sixth-grade camp!

Still, I was nervous because camp is a week-long trip and I had only slept over for one night at a time. I had strong faith and high hopes. If camp was going to go well, then I would have to go into it with an extremely positive attitude. The next few weeks passed very quickly, and sixth-grade camp was around the corner. It was the biggest test to all of my months in therapy. It was my time to prove to myself that those months had all been worth it.

On that Monday morning, my class loaded our bags into a large bus. When our stuff was packed, we all walked onto the bus. The whole school came out to wave to us as the bus started to pull off and drive away. It was a fun moment.

Once we were on the road, the mask came up. If I was going to make it through the week, nobody could see any insecurities from me. I had decided that. I would not let my guard down in front of all my friends.

We arrived at the campsite and settled into our cabins. We started the activities very quickly, which ended up being a great bonus because we could fit more activities into the day. That meant we would be really tired by the end of the day, so hopefully falling asleep would be easy.

My prediction was correct. I was exhausted by the end of the day, and I fell asleep without any struggles at all.

When I woke up the next morning, I was ready to have fun. The mask was coming down, and I was starting to act like the real me. I knew that each day would be just as exhausting as the first, and I knew that as each night passed, it could only become easier to fall asleep.

As each day came and went, I felt proud. I usually don't feel pride for myself, but I was really happy with the result of my work in therapy. It was a good feeling.

The camping trip as a whole ended up being a piece of cake! My anxiety had me planning for the worst, but everything ended up being amazing. My transition from never attending sleepovers to spending four nights in a cabin away from home was extremely smooth. I had doubts at times, but I overcame my fears. There were only two months left of sixth grade after the camping trip ended. Summer was coming, and I was ready for it. Things could only go up from there. At least, that's what I thought.

Everybody else may have been asleep,
but God was with me.
I knew it.

—Christine XP

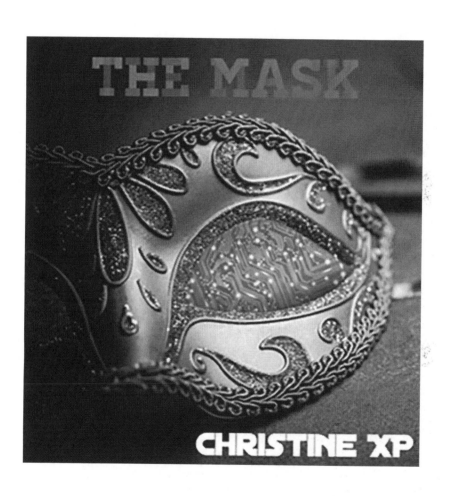

THE MASK

CHRISTINE XP

My Brain XP Friends:
"The Mask" takes you through the ups
and downs in life as the internal masks that
guard our true selves are ripped away.
Do you have a mask, too?

Christine XP

Thoughts?

Check out the Brain XP website for my current blog,
music, videos & performances

www.brainxpproject.com

Is It Me?

Is it me
feeling so sad
crying in my sleep
feeling so bad
starting to grieve
Lord please
I need you
I need you

Is it me
that's starting to crash
is it me
that just won't last
and I know that not all prayers get answered
in a direct way

but I know that nothing will ever feel the same
but I know that nothing will ever feel the same

Is it me
left behind
is it me
that's just wasting their time
Lord I need an answer
I know I should be here
where are you
where are you

and I see, and I see
who I can be
but Lord I just can't tell if I'm already broke

Chapter Three

Is It Me?

The summer after sixth grade was supposed to be amazing. The school year ended on a great note, and I really didn't have any worries after the camp experience was completely behind me.

The problem is life doesn't always go perfectly right or become the reality you are expecting. The amazing picture that I had created in my mind for the summer after sixth grade was simply not the way it turned out. Unexpected things happened, and I found myself in tough circumstances.

At the time, my free time was completely dedicated to playing soccer. I had been playing since kindergarten, and I had been on a competitive club soccer team for two years. I had great friends on my team and a great coach.

The soccer club I played for was fairly small, which I really liked because the positive philosophy of the club was enforced. I loved the philosophy because it made me feel like I was a big contributor to the team. It told me winning was not everything. Having fun and skill improvement were the most important aspects of the game. Good sportsmanship was essential as well. I was only twelve years old during the summer following sixth grade. I knew I needed a club exactly like this one if I wanted to really take my soccer abilities to the next level.

I later found out that my club would be merging with another local soccer club to create a new club. It would be much larger, and we would all have to try out again in order to make the new team. I also found out that my coach would not be coaching for the new club. I was honestly pretty upset this was happening. Nothing was bad about all this, but then and now, it is hard for me to adapt to change. Transitions are a huge weakness for me. The lack of control I feel when changes are happening around and to me really increases my anxieties.

Because I had friends connected to the club, I decided to try out again for the new team. I ended up making the team and some of my really good friends also made it. It was a good feeling to know that I was already familiar with some of my teammates. There were, of course, new faces to the team, but everyone seemed to get along reasonably well. We were all playing together on the same team, but many of us didn't really know each other so the initial rhythm wasn't smooth. I felt apprehensive not knowing all the team members or what to expect from the new coaches.

Shortly after I made the team, I started having doubts. It had only been a few months since I had gotten out of the cast from my second broken ankle injury, so I hadn't been playing consistently for a while. We had a tournament coming up, and I still felt wobbly on my foot from that injury. As my team warmed up for the first game of the tournament, I felt my ankle worsening. I didn't think I could play because it was too unstable. I became emotional and started to cry. I went to my new coach to tell him I couldn't play because of my ankle. I sat out and watched the first game. The tournament was two hours away from home, so I couldn't get much help for my ankle. There was no medical support at the tournament. We just put ice on it hoping it would be better in the morning. I wanted to give my ankle some rest without the pressure of standing on it. I did not have much time to recuperate before I needed to get ready for the next game.

I got to the second game in the morning and tried to warm up with the team, but my ankle was still acting up. I truly tried my best to play. I didn't want to let my friends down by not playing or playing terribly while at the same time damaging my ankle even more. I decided to talk to the coach.

My communication with my new coach was not ideal. I didn't quite know how to express all the concerns I had. Because it was so close to game time I simply told him, "I can't play." By that time, I was certain I couldn't play because I had broken the same ankle twice, and I knew the amount of pain it took for me to realize that something felt really wrong.

My coach tried to play me anyway. Because we had not worked together for very long, I think the communication between us was just off. He may have been trying to encourage me to get out on the field or maybe not. I didn't really know, but I started to panic. I could not play, and he could not push me into it. The anxiety started to creep up and the mask came out.

I sat on the sideline and took off my cleats and shin guards to make sure he was aware I would not be playing. I felt so sad. The philosophy I once knew had completely disappeared in my eyes. The players should have been the number one priority, and I did not feel that was the case.

After the tournament was over, my mom and I drove back to San Diego. I spent a lot of time thinking about my teammates, my coaches, and my love for soccer. It just didn't seem like the right mix. As we drove home, I started crying. I didn't know what to do. I didn't feel like I was a part of the team, but soccer was so important to me.

My mom helped me realize some different aspects. I was not having fun, and I was wasting lots of my time committing myself to a place where I didn't feel welcome. I also realized that I should only play for myself. I should not play for a coach. I should not play for my parents. I should not play for anyone but myself, because soccer was that important to me! On this new team, nothing seemed to be about me anymore. It felt like I was playing almost because I had to. I realized that no one was making me play. If it wasn't the right fit for me, then so be it. Ultimately, my parents decided to pull me off the team.

My feelings were mixed. I felt somewhat relieved, but also incredibly distraught. I was just so scared that if I left the team my friendships would change. I was sad. I felt so misunderstood as a person. It was as simple as that. Some things needed to happen and were worth it. I couldn't help but cry though. I didn't want the situation to end like that.

I picked myself up and continued on. I needed to push through and keep going. Life could not be blocked off forever.

I was not used to being so emotional. I think I was particularly upset because I wanted the summer to be great, and it really wasn't. I wanted a great follow-up to sixth grade and all my accomplishments from therapy, but the great follow-up never came.

It was a good feeling to know that I was already familiar with some of my teammates. There were, of course, new faces to the team, but everyone seemed to get along reasonably well.

—Christine XP

My Brain XP Friends:
"Is It Me?" This song and chapter share a part of my life that was filled with uncertainty and vulnerability. I wrote the lyrics to help myself realize that my depression was real, but also to assure myself that I could overcome it.
Do these lyrics ring true for you?

Christine XP

Thoughts?

Check out the Brain XP website for my current blog,
music, videos & performances

www.brainxpproject.com

"Beautifull" of Love

I've been asking for quite a while
what's it gonna' take to make you smile
tell me a little secret about you-why are you so shy
I see your face as you count the days as they go by
but you don't even care you're stuck in a stare
you're sad and I don't know why
it's nothing more it's nothing less
I just wanna' see you smile again

Because you're beautiful
and there's no such thing as worthless and girl
you deserve to hear that
you're beautiful
"beautifull" of love "beautifull" of love
you're "beautifull" of love "beautifull" of love

I've been thinking 'bout it for some time
something's just wrong something's not right
'cuz I know this girl she was as bright as the world
all she's got left are cuts, scars, and burns
people just left her alone
she's facing life all on her own
and she won't pick up the phone
I just need to tell her

Because you're beautiful
and there's no such thing as worthless and girl
you deserve to hear that
you're beautiful
"beautifull" of love "beautifull" of love
you're "beautifull" of love "beautifull" of love

Chapter Four

"Beautifull" of Love

My self-esteem had declined dramatically by the time I started seventh grade. I had always spent so much of my time with my friends on the soccer field that leaving the team really threw me off. Bonds I had formed with the girls on the team were slowly breaking simply because I was not around them anymore. I was honestly upset with myself. This was all happening because I had felt like the team was not healthy for me. I could have stayed on the team, but I felt unimportant and misunderstood whenever I spent time with them. It was over. My confidence was drowning, and once again, the mask came up.

I needed to suck it up and move on. Besides, seventh grade was starting, and I had a fresh, clean slate. I knew I could bounce back quickly by spending time with my friends at school.

Being a seventh-grader was supposed to be fun. It meant you were the cool older kids. My school was pre-k through eighth grade and I had been there since preschool. I had almost made my way to the very top. The little kindergartners looked up to me and I loved playing with them during lunch or after school. As I thought about the good times of earlier school years, I began to feel my own sense of importance again. I was feeling hopeful for the new school year.

The first month of seventh grade went pretty well. I was off to a fresh start and felt excited about the potential for this to be a great year.

Unfortunately, the feeling of excitement only lasted for that first month. It died out at the end of September. The distressful, unhappy world of last school year stared right in my face. I could not get away from the ugliness of my reality.

I realize that reality was probably not as bad as it seemed to me. I just knew I was terribly sad and that nobody wanted to hang out with a person who was sad and down all the time. I slowly separated from my friendships. It was the same thing that had happened with my soccer team. I didn't know what to do.

I struggled through October, my mask held directly in front of my face. The last thing I needed was to let my guard down in front of all my friends. I had a certain amount of pride that I would not swallow, so I kept every issue to myself. Issues build up and, in my case, they built up fast.

My mask was special to me. It was literally like my best friend. When I was nervous, anxious, angry, or upset I could count on my mask to get me out of it. It was always there. I was hiding from life and I didn't even know it. I was hiding behind my mask. My mask had become my replacement for God. I didn't even realize it. I had not talked to God for months. I don't think I had talked to Him since sixth-grade camp and that had been six months earlier. I knew God was what I needed to count on, not my mask.

I did what I felt was necessary. I took down my invisible mask and set my emotions free.

As October ended, I attended school daily. I held on to the new realizations about my life and who I should be relying on. I trusted God to get me out of the sad pit I was stuck in. I didn't know His plan, but I was counting on Him.

I sat at lunch on a cloudy day in November by myself at the outside lunch tables. The wind was blowing, but it wasn't cold enough for me to have to move around to stay warm, so I just sat there. I looked around and saw everybody walking and playing games. I continued to sit there. I was contemplating what my real issue was. I had great friendships. The only reason they were falling apart was because I was so down. It's hard to hang out with someone who is unable to have fun. I understood that, but I also understood that I was in a horrible place. I needed people to talk to and confide in. My communication skills were falling apart. I didn't know how to convey the message that I really needed my friends and that I was not purposely turning away from them.

As I sat at the lunch table watching my friends from a distance, I came to the realization that something deeper had to be going on with me. I had spent my whole life surrounded by these people. I knew that our friendships were still there. They were just on pause for the moment. I had fought with these friends, but I also had amazing memories with them. They were lifelong friendships and couldn't possibly have the power to make me this sad. I knew my friends were not responsible for this kind of sadness.

It was right then that I realized I simply didn't know what was wrong. I could not pinpoint it. Not only was I sad, I felt so incredibly alone. My anxiety was standing over me all the time. I never raised my hand in class anymore. I never spoke unless I was spoken to. I never participated in anything at all. I withdrew from everything. I needed help, but I didn't want it. I didn't want to bother someone. I didn't want them to waste their time on me because I felt sad. I just didn't.

I sat there by myself all through lunch. When the bell rang to end the period, I started walking toward my classroom. The mask was down, and it stayed down. I needed to face my battles without hiding.

I walked toward my classmates but didn't make any eye contact. Then I slowed down. The worst feeling came over me. I needed to cry, but I really didn't want to. The mask would have prevented all of this, but God was telling me to get it out. I fought it. I really did. I could not win this battle. I stood there and just lost it.

I looked down and tried to act like I was not crying, but it was too obvious. My friends walked over and asked what was wrong. What was I supposed to tell them? I had just had a powerful insight. But now realized I had no clue what was wrong with me. But there I was, crying without the slightest bit of knowledge as to why tears were streaming down my face.

My teacher called me over and talked to me. I was honest with him. He told me that he had noticed this buildup of sadness for the past month, but whenever he tried to talk to me, I had acted as if nothing was wrong. This time I said it, "I feel alone. I feel sad, and I don't know why!" He cheered me up with a pep talk, but the sadness and loneliness were still with me. We did the best we could for the time being.

On a good note, my teacher's encouragement lifted me up and I felt better for the rest of the day. I had caught a break, no pun intended. The school break for Christmas vacation would be starting the following day and school would be out.

The only real joy I had had over these past few months came from music. During the summer before seventh grade, I purchased a guitar and taught myself how to play some basic chords. I also started to write lyrics as I experienced my emotional downs. The raw truth came out in those lyrics and with the guitar I turned them into songs. I would come home each day after school and play my guitar. I shut the door, wrote down a line, and played the line. I did this over and over until the song was complete. Over time, the songs piled up into a really nice collection. I started to feel that my songwriting was the only thing I was good at, but I wasn't completely sure about that. I easily spent at least an hour a day in my room playing and writing.

On weekends, I would be in there hours longer. It was the only thing that helped me feel less sad, so it made sense to me to spend time doing something I enjoyed. My room and music became my happy place and I could not find that anywhere else.

Eventually, there was a backlash—my self-isolation. I never wanted to come out of my bedroom. My healthy pleasure was causing an unhealthy experience for me by inhibiting my involvement in the outside world. It was Christmas break in the seventh grade. I had two weeks to piece myself back together before I would continue tackling the monster that school had become in the outside world.

My mask had become my replacement for God. I didn't even realize it.

I knew God was what I needed to count on, not my mask.

—Christine XP

Beautifull of Love

CHRISTINE XP

My Brain XP Friends:
"Beautifull of Love" is really just a play on words. We are all beautiful, and we are all full of love. I wrote the lyrics of this song to remind myself of that. This chapter helped me realize that my depression would not bring me to a quitting point.
Do you feel beautiful?

Christine XP

Thoughts?

Check out the Brain XP website for my current blog,
music, videos & performances

www.brainxpproject.com

"Babygirl"

I'm not lucky I'm blessed
get your facts straight
I don't care what you do next
'cuz you're not the first to say
"Babygirl" I never meant
to put you in this place
ooh "Babygirl" is there anyway
(we can fix this
I'll buy the tools
anything you like
I said no we're through)

He says "Babygirl"
you won't get hurt
he says "babygirl"
I'll never treat you like dirt

I'm not just talking 'bout this
'cuz there's too many girls treated like this
I don't care if you can fix it
go ahead and try but I won't listen
what's the point where's the trust
I don't play this game
you can keep on asking
but I'll never look at you the same
(who's to blame I don't care
wipe that pout and puppy dog stare
the truth comes out
I don't have to dare)

Chapter Five

"Babygirl"

Christmas break was an eye-opener for me. I usually experienced my major emotional problems when I was at school. This is where, on a daily basis, I withdrew from my friends, fought anxiety, and had bouts of sadness and tears. My house, especially my bedroom with my music, had always felt like my "safe" place. But over the two-week break from school, I started to feel overcome with sadness in my own home. It felt like my safe place had disappeared.

I started doubling the amount of time I spent alone in my room. I was productive by either playing or listening to music, but I was hardly ever conversing with people.

Traditionally, my family always spent time together enjoying Christmas. We drove by decorated houses and drank hot chocolate. We invited extended family over to hang out with us. We set out cookies for Santa on Christmas Eve and we opened presents early on Christmas morning. It was special to me. I wanted every Christmas to be spent with my family following the same traditions we had developed over time.

This Christmas was different. I didn't feel like spending time with my family. I didn't feel like seeing Christmas lights. I didn't feel like opening presents. I didn't feel like doing anything at all. I just didn't see the point anymore. I became less and less interested in everything.

I remember one of the games my family loved to play was an

59

outdoor game we called Soccer Foursquare. We all walked to a field not far from my house to play. My brother was by far the best player, but I had a lot of fun competing. We played this game almost every day during Christmas breaks while my brother and I were out of school. It gave us more time together.

I realized things were changing inside me during this seventh-grade Christmas break. I no longer wanted to participate in games with my family. I couldn't find anything to motivate me or drive me to get out and have fun.

The first few times I told my family I would rather stay home than play Soccer Foursquare with them, they were fine. They didn't question me. They just gave me my space.

I'll never forget the look in my brother's eyes when I refused to play for the fourth or fifth time. I honestly believe he had a mask of his own at times because I couldn't always read him, but I knew he could tell something was wrong with me.

If things didn't start to look up, I had a bad feeling that the people I loved would end up getting hurt worse than me. I could fight. I knew that. They could fight their own battles as well. Watching someone else hurting is far worse for me than being hurt myself.

I thought I just needed an easy fix, something to give me a quick way out of this isolation and sadness. I knew I was far from getting better because my heart hurt. That is one of the worst feelings I've ever experienced. I can go to the doctor and get a cast on my leg to heal a bone. I can go to the doctor to get stitches to heal a deep cut. I can identify many different kinds of problems and discover good solutions within a reasonable amount of time. But I could not go to the doctor to fix a sad heart and I had no way of knowing how long these feelings would last. That is what scared me.

Christmas break was full of realizations, but nothing was improving. I still couldn't understand what was happening to me.

When school started again in January, I did my best to work hard and get through each day. Those were my only goals at the time. I didn't care enough to want to hang out with friends. I didn't care enough to set long term goals for the future. I didn't care about a good future for myself. I began to like myself less and less. I was not pretty or smart. I was not a good athlete or a good friend. I was just another body in the crowd. I was unnoticeable. That was what I believed.

The problem was that I couldn't get through a day at school without crying. I tried so hard to keep my composure, but I couldn't. My teacher told me that if things didn't start to get better, he would have to call my parents to let them know that I had been crying and acting sad on a regular basis at school.

I couldn't let that happen. I needed space and to be left alone. If my parents found out how bad things were going at school, they would put me back into counseling which would force me to talk. I hated talking. Nothing I said was worth being heard anyway.

The truth is I was blessed to have someone looking out for me at school. My teacher was kind and patient with me, but I knew I was not going to be magically happy. Soon, he would be calling my parents.

I was doing homework one day after school when I heard my mom's phone ring. I pretended to work, but I was really eavesdropping on her conversation. By the way she was talking and by what she was saying, I knew it was my teacher on the other line. My heart dropped. I felt like my whole world had just blown up. I didn't want my parents to be involved.

I stopped eavesdropping and went back to work. I didn't care anymore. I knew everything would be out in the open, and I hated that. At age twelve, I was already such a private person. My feelings were meant to be kept to myself, but that wasn't going to be allowed anymore. I was going to have to explain my feelings to my parents and if I wouldn't talk to them, then a therapist would make me talk. I didn't know this for sure, but I had a pretty solid sense that was what was going to happen.

When my mom got off the phone, she came into the living room where I was working. She calmly asked me how school had gone that day. I pushed it off and said it was fine. She told me that my teacher had called and was concerned about me. After she told me what they had discussed, I acknowledged that things at school could be better, but I gave no explanations, excuses, or information about all that was happening to me emotionally. The details were meant to stay with me and I planned to keep them with me.

My mom brought up therapy next. I knew it was coming and I cringed at the thought of it. I didn't need anybody. I didn't want anybody to help me fix myself. I believed that if I was strong enough, I would get better all on my own.

When I had gone to therapy before, I felt satisfied with it when it was over because I was able to go on sleepovers with friends and attend the sixth-grade camp out. I stopped going to that therapist after I met my goal and did not ever plan to go to therapy again. I felt very negative on the subject of going back to therapy when my mom suggested it would be a good idea in my current situation of having continual sad feelings that became so intense at school. I had a negative mindset as I started out in my first session. But, by my second therapy session, my negativity grew into feelings of desperation. I badly needed to find out what was wrong with me.

Toward the end of January, I began noticing shadows when the sun wasn't even out. At first, I didn't think too much of it, so I kept it to myself. Later, another odd thing happened at home. I was walking in the hallway past my room and saw one of my stuffed animals sitting on my bed. The stuffed animal was a black and white panda, but it looked different. It looked completely dark, like it had changed colors. I only saw it at a glance as I was walking by the door to my room. I stopped, stepped back, and looked at it again. This time it looked normal. I found these encounters strange and a little scary. I decided I would force myself to talk to my therapist about them.

At my next session, I told my therapist about the shadows and darkness. When I left the session, my confidence was shaken. What had happened could not be normal.

After that session, my therapist contacted my mom. The result was that now we had to go find my third therapist! This therapist gave my mom two new referrals to other places for therapy and said the program I was in with her was not the right fit for me.

"Not the right fit for me?" What was that supposed to mean? I was desperate for help, and now the person who said she would help me suddenly decided to turn me over to another therapist. I knew there had to be a good reason for my therapist to suggest this change, but what could it be? I felt so stuck, confused, and scared because I could not figure out what that reason might be.

Shortly after the new referrals were given to us, my mom and I went to see one of the recommended therapists. This new therapist said the same thing. She told us that she was "not the right fit for me."

I couldn't comprehend the thought that there was a "fit" for therapy. I thought I was supposed to get my feelings out and see what the therapist thought I should do. That was it. Apparently, I was wrong.

Our next effort was to find the location of a special clinic that was a psychosis prevention center. This was our final referral. It felt like this clinic was my last chance to get the help I needed.

My mom and I arrived at the center and began filling out paperwork. One of the therapists who worked at the center came out to meet with us. He brought us into a private room and gave me this incredibly long evaluation. He asked me so many questions about my feelings and any unusual things going on in my life. I literally thought it was never going to end, but when it finally did, I felt like this therapist really understood me. He asked the questions so calmly, and he was patient with me when I had a hard time forming my thoughts into words.

I was still scared to talk to someone completely new about my feelings, but something seemed right about this psychosis prevention center. The one thing I was not sure about was what "psychosis" actually meant. I had no clue, but I was determined to find out!

With a little bit of research, I began to understand that psychosis is a mental illness and is related to losing a sense of reality. I had been losing my sense of reality when I saw the shadows that were not there. It was the same thing when I saw the stuffed panda completely dark. I learned that these experiences are called "hallucinations" and they are the primary symptoms of psychosis. A person with psychosis can have different kinds of hallucinations because they happen when the part of the brain that controls the five senses is not working correctly. My first two hallucinations were visual, meaning I *saw* things that were not real—the shadows and the dark panda. Hallucinations always seem totally real to the person who is having them. I felt pretty sure that nobody around me was seeing what I was seeing. When I finished my research, I was very curious to hear what the therapist learned from his evaluation of me.

If I had psychosis, it did not feel like an illness to me. When I learned that the whole point of the center was to prevent teens and young adults from experiencing psychosis, I understood that I didn't actually have it. I was basically in the very early stages of developing psychosis. The treatment program at this center would help me by providing individual therapy, occupational therapy, family therapy, multi-family group therapy, and other services. They also had a medical specialist on staff who could prescribe medication to help *prevent* and control psychotic symptoms. All of these services were in place so that clients like me could learn to take care of themselves and improve their mental health with the goal of stabilizing their lives.

I really hoped the center would accept me into their program. I could see myself getting better there.

After reviewing the evaluation at my next appointment, the therapist looked straight at my mom and said with complete confidence and honesty that he believed the program was a "great fit for me!" I was scared and hopeful at the same time. For the first time, I realized that there really was a reason for the way I felt. I had to accept that it would take work to get better with this program.

I finally had professional support behind me as well as support from my family. Little pieces of hope and confidence began to bubble up inside me.

Meanwhile, I was still going to school. I continued to cry every day. My teacher was still looking out for me, which told me a lot. No matter how alone I may have felt before, I knew I was not alone now. I had my teacher, my family, a good therapist, and a program that was "a great fit for me!"

Unfortunately, my judgment was still off because of all the hatred I had for myself. On Valentine's Day, I woke up feeling so sad and confused. I blamed myself for the emotional upheaval I was going through. Thinking my unhappy, chaotic circumstances were my own fault made me angry. I just didn't get it. How could anyone love me when I didn't love myself?

Despite feeling this way, I got out of bed that morning and got ready for school. Before I went downstairs, I grabbed a pair of scissors and sat on my bed. Because I was so sad and angry, I wanted an immediate release from the mixed-up emotions I was feeling. Without thinking, I took the scissors and slashed them against the inside of my wrist. When blood didn't come out, I became angrier. I thought I was so dumb that I couldn't even cut my wrists right! I did it again and this time my wrist began bleeding.

When blood started to come out from the scissor cut, I got scared. I was shocked that I had hurt myself. I didn't find any pleasure in seeing the blood or feeling the pain, even though that was originally what I wanted to have happen.

I went down the stairs and showed my mom what I had done. I was crying. I didn't want to harm anything or anybody including myself. I told her it just kind of happened because of all the sadness and anger I was feeling.

My mom helped me bandage the bleeding wrist and gave me the option to stay home from school. The weird thing about me is that I always feel driven to overcome if I am in dire straits. Since I was struggling at school, I was determined to keep going until I was satisfied that improvements were being made. I was not satisfied, so I told my mom I would go to school.

It was a very hot day, but I kept my sweatshirt on to make sure nobody saw my bandage. I actually almost made it through that whole day at school without crying. I managed to compose myself until the very end of the day. When the dismissal bell rang, I lost it. Everyone was leaving the classroom, but I started crying. I didn't know exactly why, but I was just so upset and confused. I had no idea what I was doing with my life. This may sound dramatic, but I felt lost in the sense that I didn't know what I wanted out of life anymore. The feeling of hopelessness overwhelmed me. That really hurt.

My teacher talked to me in the classroom, but I didn't explain anything. I was done. My mom picked me up a few minutes later. I immediately went to my room to listen to music when we got home. I needed to shut out the world.

As I took my iPod out and started to put my headphones on, something was very wrong. On the black screen of my iPod, there were finger smudges. The finger smudges created a clear image of a demonic face. I rubbed my fingers against the screen to get the face to go away and then threw the iPod down on my bed. When I came back to my room later that evening, the screen was absolutely fine again. Seeing the demonic face was a new visual hallucination for me. It was much scarier than the first ones. I didn't understand it at the time, but my illness was becoming more serious.

Valentine's Day finally passed, and I went to school the next day. As I sat in the chair at my desk, I began to hear faint whispers. I tried to ignore them because I could tell that nobody else heard them. I assumed this was just the next issue I would have to deal with. I had seen dark shadows that nobody else could see, so it didn't completely surprise me that I was hearing whispers that nobody else could hear.

I sat at my desk, feeling annoyed. The whispers were more bothersome to me than something I worried about. They eventually died down and I started back to work. Next, I began to hear two distinct voices saying things only I could hear. These voices were different from the whispers and I had never heard them before. I didn't recognize them as voices of anyone I knew. They sounded mischievous with a tone of laughter built into them. They told me that I was not pretty and that I was a bad person. That was it, just one brief episode of voices. I didn't have any more trouble for the rest of the day and was able to concentrate and do my school work.

The next day, those same voices were back. They weren't strong enough to block out the sound of everything and everyone around me. Listening to them say mean things about me did become annoying–especially when I already felt like I wasn't pretty or a good person. I didn't need them to remind me. I already believed it.

I tried to think of the demons and voices as just a distraction that I should be able to ignore or adapt to. I started to hear them less and less even though they were still talking. Whatever the voices were, they must have caught on to my pattern of ignoring them because they began talking louder. It got to a point where I was in my own world. I never said anything back to them, but these voices were unstoppable. It went far past a simple annoyance or distraction for me. I started having a hard time distinguishing what was real and what was not.

All during this time, I was seeing my new therapist on a weekly basis and had started taking medication. The process of adjusting to new or additional medications is incredibly slow. I had a hard time getting over the fact that even one medication takes at least a few weeks or even longer before you see if it has the desired effect. I started out with a very low dosage of just one medication, so I was basically waiting for the process to continue while the doctor adjusted my medication regimen over several weeks to determine the best dosage and combination of medications for my condition.

In the meantime, I continued to struggle. I was talking to my teacher in our classroom after school when something very strange came over me. I could see my teacher and I could hear his voice clearly, but for some reason I didn't believe it was him. I swore it was the demon I had seen in the smudges on my phone. I didn't see the demon around my teacher, but I sensed that somehow the demon had taken him over. I realized that I had lost all understanding of what was happening with my teacher. I was finally able to leave the classroom and walk over to my after-school daycare program. As I was walking away from my classroom, one of my friends came over to me. From that moment on, everything was fine. Everything around my friend and me was the way it had always been. I looked back at my teacher from a distance, and I knew it was him. My mom was supposed to pick me up a few hours later, but she came early. She picked me up just a few minutes after the incident.

I couldn't help what was going on, but it became obvious to me that I was being watched. The demon and the beings behind the voices were watching me. The faculty at school were watching me, and my parents were watching me. I felt like there really was no safe space anymore, and again, I blamed myself.

As I adapted more and more every day to just get through school, the voices evolved into a visual form. I mostly heard them, but occasionally I saw them. There were three demonic beings that I would hear or see. There was one main demon and his two demonic sidekicks. The main demon had a very low deep voice and was not playful. The two demonic sidekicks had cheery and light playful voices but would say very rude things. The sidekicks were always together. I never saw or heard just one sidekick. The main demon, however, would talk or come at his own pleasure. The sidekicks did anything and everything the main demon told them to do. I had to admit they made an interesting team, but they were unkind and hurtful. The main demon was the scariest of the three because he literally took on the role of the devil. Evil was written all over him.

I didn't want to give them power by naming them. My mom was having a hard time keeping track of which demon was which, so instead, I numbered them. I called the main demon One. The sidekicks were called Two and Three. It helped me as well because I could explain my situations better to my mom and my therapist. Power was not given to them, but the three of us could comprehend better what I

69

was experiencing. It was an all-around good idea to label them.

School was by far the most difficult aspect of my life, but I always went. I needed to prove to myself that I could do it. Day after day life got harder and harder for me, but I was determined to keep fighting. The only good trait I felt I had left was my determination, and it would be the key to my success.

I finally had professional support behind me as well as support from my family. Little pieces of hope and confidence began to bubble up inside me.

—Christine XP

My Brain XP Friends:

"Babygirl" brings you into a very dark place in my life. While I was having episodes of psychosis, I was often called "babygirl" by the demons who haunted me. There was nothing sweet about the phrase when I heard it, so I spell the title my way. Not right! Just wrong! The words were always uttered in a mean sounding tone. I wrote this song to release the negativity involved in my relationships with these demons. It represents the value of trust and my hesitancy to invest my trust in others. Is it hard for you to trust others?

Christine XP

Thoughts?

Check out the Brain XP website for my current blog,
music, videos & performances

www.brainxpproject.com

May 13th

Been talking about something
you won't believe but it happened
scared for my life no question
these little demons were stalking
left after school daylight
doubting I'd be home that night
counting my breaths
not sure if they'd be my last

You've got me screaming
In my mind it was a scream zone
You've got me praying
Don't leave me alone

Aye aye aye
what's my name
I'm not who you've made me out to be
Aye aye aye
I'm not crazy
I'm not who you've made me out to be

Don't act like you know me when you don't
Don't act like you know me when you don't

Got me thinking I'm crazy
In my head somewhere, I know I'm okay
Got me thinking unwisely
Now I know it's 'cuz you despise me
Not sure of my thoughts
I knew where I was but now I am lost
You said you'd never leave me
But I was already in too deep

Chapter Six

May 13th

My determination was put to the test every day as I continued to battle in school. In April of my seventh-grade year, my class was scheduled to go on a one-day field trip with the eighth grade. We were going on a bus from our school in San Diego to a museum in Los Angeles.

I was nervous, but I wasn't scared. I knew if I tried really hard I could sit through a few hours on the bus ride to get there. I knew I could manage looking around the museum for another few hours. I could also sit through the bus ride back home. I was fine with that.

What I didn't know was whether the voices or demons would come and try to shatter my focus on reality. I needed to prove to myself that I could make it through the day. During the field trip, I would have nowhere to escape. I would either be sitting on the bus or touring the museum. I needed to stay calm. The one good thing about the trip was that my teacher would be there. If anything went wrong, I had him to help me.

On the day of the field trip, we all got onto the bus. I sat in the very back by myself. I was somewhat happy that I was sitting alone because I wouldn't have to talk to anybody else. I would be able to focus completely on staying calm.

The bus ride was not bad at all. I was able to sit and just look out the window the whole time, which took my mind off the pain and anxiety I was feeling in my heart. My thoughts were blocked off and my composure was on point. The first part of the trip riding the bus was a success.

I don't remember much about touring the museum. My mind was on other matters. I began to physically feel the demons surround me. I couldn't see or hear them, but I could sense them. I knew they were around. My anxiety was over the top. I prayed that God would make time move faster.

I could barely think. All I could do was follow my classmates as we moved through the museum. The only coping skill I knew was to ignore my feelings and sensations of the demons' presence.

I stared at the ceilings of the museum because I thought the demons were watching me from weird angles above me. I kept trying to ignore them and somehow managed to. While my visit to the museum was not a grand success, I gave it my best effort. At least I think that is what my mask showed on the outside to those around me. On the inside, I felt sadness oozing through me because I had failed.

I started to feel scared. I knew there were a few more hours left before I would be back home. I would be trapped on the bus the whole way home. I tried to hide my fear but feeling afraid shows all over my face. No mask can hide it.

As the bus pulled up and my classmates started piling into it, I realized I was terrified to get back on the bus. I put on my brave face and walked onto the bus as if everything was perfectly fine. I sat down in the very back, by myself again, next to the window that had become my best friend. My eyes were glued to that window. I made no eye contact with any living being on the bus. Just the window. No distractions. No interruptions. I needed to do this on my own. My focus was in charge and it had to prevent the fear from taking control.

As time slowly passed, looking out the window stopped working.

I could see cars as I stared out the window. Because the bus was tall, they were below where I was sitting. As I looked down at the other cars, I saw one of the demons just riding along on top of a car. When I saw him, he looked straight at me. He had a funny look on his face that gave me the impression he was laughing at me. I knew the demon was one of the sidekicks. He appeared to be playful in nature. As he stared at me, he waved. Car after car passed and the demon reappeared on every car—one after another. I surprised myself when I didn't scream out or start crying. Afterwards, I wondered whether I was beginning to get used to having hallucinations.

I looked away from the window for a while, hoping the demon would disappear. When I looked out again, the demon was gone. Because we were finally getting closer to school, with no demons in sight, I was able to relax a little before our arrival.

We got back to school, and I went home shortly after that. Since no one really knew what I had experienced on the bus ride, I decided to keep it to myself. It had been a very hard day and I was exhausted. I just hoped the next day would be better.

After the field trip, my mental health was far from ideal. My birthday was coming up soon. On May 17, I would be thirteen years old. I felt desperate to get rid of the demons and knew I was completely vulnerable to their appearances. Stress and anxiety were my constant companions, keeping me always on guard.

On May 13th, I was at school and it was just four days before my birthday. It was close to the end of the day, but there was still a good hour left before the dismissal bell would ring. During class, I heard the demon leader begin to speak to me. He promised me that he and his sidekicks would leave forever under one condition—that I run away.

He gave me no details. He didn't say where I needed to run or for how long I should stay away. He just told me to run away. If I did, he said, "We will be gone forever."

My feelings of desperation ramped all the way up. It would be wrong to run away. It was not an idea I would have ever thought of doing myself. I was still just twelve years old and no one would be around to look out for me or help me if things went wrong. It was a bad idea all the way around. Still, I wanted the demons gone. I wanted my life to be mine again. If I ran away, would the demon leader keep his promise to leave and never come back?

When the bell rang to end the school day, I was supposed to go to the school's daycare on campus. My mom was going to pick me up at daycare a little bit later and then we would go to my guitar lesson.

However, instead of going to daycare, I walked straight out of the school. I planned to walk a few blocks away from the school, so the demons would leave as promised.

I walked for a while, but I grew tired. I was carrying my backpack full of textbooks, my binder, and my guitar in its case. The demons were still talking to me, so I knew that they hadn't left yet. I needed a break. So, I stopped at a bus stop and sat on the bench for a few minutes, but soon afterwards started walking again.

It was very hot that day, so I walked another few blocks to the library because it was air-conditioned. I began to worry because the demons still hadn't left, and I had reached an area of town that I wasn't as familiar with.

Because I was so nervous and worried, I tried to take my mind off things. Since I was at the library, I took out my books and did my homework. Strangely, it helped a bit. I was able to focus on homework and not think about the demons for a while. Once I was finished, I decided I should keep walking. I picked up all my things and left the library.

It was still very hot outside. I was thirsty and had no water. I noticed a small coffee shop nearby and walked over there. I bought a cold drink with the few dollars I had in my backpack. As I sat down to start drinking it, I pulled out my phone and noticed that it was turned off. As I was looking at the screen, the demons began yelling that I couldn't use the phone.

I checked my phone anyway and found several texts and voicemails from friends and family asking where I was and if I was okay. I became terrified because I thought the demons were totally serious about not using that phone. I didn't know what to do. Not only were the demons demanding I do what they wanted, they also must have been watching me. They were not showing themselves to me, but they were close enough to see me. There was no safe place for me. I put the phone away without calling to reassure anybody. I started walking again.

I grew extremely discouraged, but I kept walking. I could not get rid of the demons. I felt like a failure and was afraid I would never stop having the hallucinations. The demons were so real. I could not out-think them.

I finally decided I would just go back to school. I headed in the direction I thought the school was located, but I was off. I ended up in a military neighborhood I had never been in. Now, I was completely lost!

At that point, I knocked on someone's door to ask for directions, but the man who answered the door had never heard of my school. He couldn't help me.

I sat down on a curb to think. It was right then I realized the demons were gone. They were no longer speaking. I couldn't see them or sense them at all. I had gotten what I wanted, but it didn't even matter because I was completely lost, alone, and unsure of what to do next.

I got up, grabbed my belongings, and started walking toward a different street in the neighborhood. I soon came to a minimart. I walked into the store and went straight to the checkout counter. I asked the workers if they knew how to get back to my school. Again, they didn't know where my school was and couldn't help me. That's when I realized my school was very small and not many people had heard of it. I needed to think of a well-known place that was near my school. I needed a landmark of some sort.

The first place I could think of was the recreational center close by my school. I asked the workers if they could give me directions to the center, but they didn't know how to get there either. Then one of the workers mentioned she knew how to get to the nearest 7-11. She didn't know if that would help me at all, but she put it out there in case it would be useful to me. I immediately told her those directions would be very helpful. I knew how to get from the 7-11 to my school because I had driven by it many times with my mom.

However, I was terrible with directions. The worker tried to explain how to get there, but I didn't know most of the street names in the area and some of the directions didn't make sense to me. I wasn't sure I would be able to find my way there, but I didn't want to be rude. So, I thanked her for the help and went on my way.

I tried to find the main street the worker had mentioned because that led out to all the other streets. It would get me out of this confusing neighborhood.

As I noticed streets that were surrounded by houses, I knew I was making progress. I was still carrying all my stuff. I was tired. I needed to use the bathroom. I refused to feel sorry for myself. I put myself in this mess and I was going to get myself out of it.

I kept walking and got closer to the main street. I looked up at all the cars passing by and knew I was finally heading the right way.

I was deep in my own thoughts, just hoping I was going to be out of this situation soon. Suddenly, a rush came over me. I was looking at a dark blue Highlander with my dad's custom license plates on it. I dropped my backpack. I dropped my binder. I dropped my guitar. I stopped looking at any other car and ran like a sprinter towards my dad's car. I had to catch his attention. I knew he had to be looking for me and I had to make sure he saw me. I waved my hands in the air until the blue car started to slow down and pull over to the curb. My dad jumped out of his car and started running toward me. I looked at him and saw tears in his eyes. We were both crying and neither one of us could stop.

We grabbed my bags and packed everything into the car. When my dad asked me what had happened, I gave him the most honest answer I could give. I said, "He told me to do it." That was all I said. My dad then asked who I was talking about. I said, "The demons."

It was in that very moment that he understood how serious an issue this had become for me. This was much bigger than a few days of crying at school. I was in danger because of the demons. I could have gotten hurt. I could have gotten even more lost than I already was. It was beginning to get dark outside and finding me would have become much more difficult. I was extremely blessed to have been found when I was. Not lucky, blessed.

When my dad and I got into the car, he called my mom to let her know he found me and I was safe. As we started to drive, I looked back at the street where I had been walking. My heart froze as I saw the demon standing there waving back at me as we pulled away. I had accomplished nothing by running away except hurt and pain to myself and everyone else who loved me and had been out looking for me.

We headed back home and a few minutes later my mom got home. I explained in detail everything that had happened. It was hard

81

to explain because we were all so emotional.

My mom told me that my friends had gone around town looking for me and even some parents were looking for me. Hearing this made me feel awful because I was responsible for causing all this emotional distress. I had taken up people's time and energy. All I had to do was go to daycare like I was supposed to do, but I didn't. I will have to live with that decision always.

There was one good thing that came out of this experience. My family and close friends truly understood how serious my condition was. If the demons hadn't existed in my mind, I would have never left school to run away. It was not in my character. I had to accept that my life was changing in many ways, but I hoped and believed that I had the power to keep my life my own. Nobody could take my hope away from me.

The whole experience was truly a scare for everybody, but again, I still had determination. I went back to school the next day and I was ready to try again. I was determined to pick up the pieces and I would do my very best never to let the demons tell me what to do again.

My birthday came a few days later and I turned thirteen years old. Maybe life was starting to look up.

The school year ended mid-June. Finally, summer was here. Starting out I knew I was depressed, but a few weeks into the summer I discovered I wasn't having as many hallucinations as I had experienced at school. Since I was at home, I was able to isolate myself and avoid communicating with others as much as possible. I'm not sure if my alone time was helping, but I felt more mentally stable during the first part of the summer.

Unfortunately, all good things must come to an end at some

point. This time it took about six weeks.

I was at home one day in late July. My brother had gone down to the field close to our house to practice baseball drills. My mom was home, and my dad was at work.

I told my mom that I was going to ride my bike down to the field where my brother was playing. As I got ready to leave the house, the demons started talking to me again. Their favorite way to hurt me was to threaten people I love. They told me I needed to run away. Again.

I thought I had learned my lesson, but in certain situations good judgment is not always the first thing that comes to mind. The demons threatened to hurt my teacher if I didn't run away.

Their demands and threats were completely real to me at the time. I absolutely believed that my teacher would get hurt if I didn't obey the demons. My only option was running away. It was as simple as that. I was in a dark place in my life and the demons knew how vulnerable I was. They took advantage of me.

I got on my bike and started riding around. I didn't know where I would run away to, so I just kept riding.

I got to a very large hill that leads into a very busy intersection. I was riding down the hill and realized I was going too fast. The hill was steeper than I had anticipated, and I was gaining speed rapidly. I grabbed my handlebar brakes, but only one of the brakes worked properly. That one brake was not strong enough to stop me because I had too much momentum.

I immediately felt the panic of a bad crash coming. Within about three seconds, I stomped my feet to the ground hoping I would come to a stop. The good brake held, but I was going so fast I flew over the handlebars and landed on the road.

God had to have been looking out for me as I sped down that hill because there was no good reason why I was not killed that day. It was an extremely busy intersection and I could have easily crashed my bike into the oncoming traffic.

When I flew off the bike, I landed next to a car that was stopped. Three women who saw the accident jumped out of their cars and ran over to help me. They got my bike out of the street, and they helped me stand up. I had cuts all over my body, but I reassured them that I was alright. I wasn't crying, didn't hit my head, and figured I was not seriously injured. I thanked them for all their help and promised I would walk my bike the rest of the way.

The women got back in their cars and I continued on. I still didn't know where I was going, so I just continued walking straight and pushing my bicycle. I kept my word to the women and didn't ride the bike after I fell.

The day I crashed marks the last time I have ridden a bike to this day. It was over three years ago, when I was thirteen. I am so blessed that God saved me that day, but the whole experience was very traumatic. I know how close I came to being killed or seriously injured. It is still a frightening memory for me—I don't think it will ever go away.

I walked with my bike for a while. Just like the first time the demons told me to run away, I ended up in a part of town that was new to me. I didn't know where I was. I was cut up and bruised and didn't have my phone with me. I felt so tired I began to wonder, what is the point in continuing?

My mom had taught me from a very young age that if I were ever to get lost, I should look for another mother. That advice stuck with me. I walked toward a neighborhood and I listened. I passed by a house that had kids shouting in the backyard. I figured a mother would be inside if her kids were outside playing. I knocked on the front door, and to my relief, a mother answered it.

I explained my situation to her and she invited me inside. She was so incredibly kind to me. I gave her my mom's cell phone number and she called my mom. She gave her the address, so my mom could come and get me. The lady cleaned up my scrapes and bandaged them. I was so grateful to her. She went out of her way to help me, but even more than that, she took loving care of me until my mom arrived. She was another one of the blessings God put in my path that day.

When my mom arrived, I got into our car and we went home. I didn't know what to think or do at that point except blame myself once again. If I could not get rid of the demons by ignoring them or obeying their commands, then I had to find some other way to combat them.

I spent the next few days thinking about how I could regain control over my life. However, another lapse in judgment soon complicated my life even more.

I started cutting my wrists again out of anger and frustration. I also began to hit my face, literally beating my face with my fist. At that point, I told my mom that I could no longer control my life and I didn't know what to do to help myself.

Safety was the number one concern and I did not feel safe. We drove to the hospital in the hope that they could provide me a safe space for the night, so my symptoms would calm down. In my mind, I was prepared to stay at the hospital with my mom and go home refreshed the next morning. That was how I envisioned this visit happening.

My vision was very wrong. When we arrived at the hospital, we waited for hours and filled out paperwork. We finally got a chance to talk to a worker there who dealt with cases involving psychosis like mine. I showed the lady my wrists and she also took a closer look at the bruises and marks on my face.

After the examination in the Emergency Room, I was escorted in a wheelchair to a different part of the hospital. I started to get really nervous. My escort brought me to a room where I sat down with another staff member. My dad had joined us by this time, so the worker spoke to all three of us.

I obviously had never experienced a situation quite like this, so I was very quiet as everybody else in the room talked.

The worker kindly explained to me what the plan was. She told me that I would be staying at the hospital, which was a safe space. The nurses would look out for me and I would be able to speak with the head doctor. I would basically be observed throughout my time there.

I asked how long I would be there and she had no definite answer. I asked where my mom could stay. She said that my parents would not be staying with me. I could feel the fear flooding through me.

I tried to explain that I didn't want to stay, but it was already too late. My parents and the hospital intake worker knew what I was experiencing in my mind and they knew my symptoms were too severe to let me go home.

I was taken to the section of the hospital where I would be staying. I was crying. I was scared. I felt so alone. I looked back at my parents as I was taken away and my mom was crying. She saw the fear and pain in my eyes. All she could do was feel the exact same fear and pain that I felt.

I entered the room I would be sleeping in. It was a room for two, but there was no one else occupying the room when I got there. I immediately went to my bed and cried myself to sleep.

About two hours after I had finally gotten to sleep, a nurse woke me up to give me my medication. I felt angry and upset. I couldn't listen to music. I couldn't have my phone. I was scared and alone. Now, my sleep had been interrupted so that I could take the medication that I didn't believe was helping me in the first place. I was done!

I was taught to be respectful, so I took the medicine without creating any issues. Then I tried to go back to sleep.

The next morning, I woke up and someone showed me where the dining room was. Before I could eat, a nurse took my blood pressure, drew blood for lab work, and gave me medication to take. When I sat down at the dining table, I filled out a piece of paper that told Food Service what I wanted to eat. The food was brought to me and I ate it. The food wasn't particularly tasty, but I only had the opportunity to eat at certain times. Breakfast, lunch, and dinner were served and there was nothing in between.

After I was finished eating, I had to show my plate to the nurse. She would track how much food I had eaten and what was still left on the plate. Every move I made was monitored. I felt more watched here at the hospital than when the demons were watching me.

The demons hadn't been bothering me since I was admitted to the hospital. I was relieved about that, but I was still scared. This whole hospital situation was new to me and I hated everything about it.

The hospital reminded me of prison. The rooms felt like prison. The rules felt like prison. The interactions with staff and other patients felt like prison. I mean even the toilets reminded me of prison! I simply did not belong there!

I stayed in the hospital for five days. Each day was worse than the one before. I longed to go home. That was all I wanted. I only got to see my parents for one hour every day during visitation. I just needed to go home. I was doing fine mentally. I was depressed, but I wasn't hallucinating. I knew I could control myself enough to be home again.

I called my mom from the hospital's phone on the fifth day. I begged her to convince the doctor that I was okay. I was upset. I was desperate. I cried and begged. I knew my mom wanted me to come home too. It was a matter of making sure the doctor was fine with me going home.

About two hours after talking to my mom, I was told that I would be going home. I was as close to being happy as a depressed kid could be. I grabbed the very few items I had with me and waited for my mom to come.

I was so relieved when I got home. I needed my music back. I needed the ability to take care of myself. I needed everyone to know I was not a threat to myself or anybody else. I needed my freedom back.

The terrible experience of going to the hospital let me know the consequences of self-harm. It was by far the worst experience I have ever had, and I didn't plan to go back. My eighth-grade year was about to begin in a few days and I wanted to start strong. I was out of the hospital and I was ready to go back to school.

In the few days I had left before school started, I decided to make a video. I never had been able to explain my condition very well to people in a face-to-face conversation. Even my family and close friends had trouble understanding what was going on with me. I thought maybe a video of me describing my difficulties would help educate them about the symptoms and complexities of a brain disorder like the one I had been diagnosed with.

The first thing I did was write down a list of questions I wanted to answer about myself and my struggles during the past two years. I planned to ask and answer the questions in the video. I then called one of my good friends to see if she would help me film the video. I had felt at ease talking with her most of the time in the past, so I figured we would be able to shoot the video together. She was completely on board with my plan. She even volunteered to bring her camera, so we would have something to film with—which was a really good idea!

I wanted to get the video done before school started. I hoped that my classmates might see it and be more comfortable around me once we were all back in the classroom together.

A couple days before the start of school, my friend came over to my house for a sleepover and to help with filming the video. She set up the camera while I went over the questions in my head. I sat on the edge of my bed holding a fidget toy and we started filming. She would ask a question, then I would give my answer. She would ask the next question and I would answer it. We went back and forth until all the questions were done. It took us most of the day to work through all the questions. When we finally went to bed, we were both very tired but felt good about what we had accomplished so far.

The next morning, we got right back to work. We downloaded what we had finished the day before onto my laptop. The next step was editing it. Since it was a straightforward video, editing wasn't too complicated.

After we finished editing, I uploaded the video to YouTube. We texted a few friends and asked them to watch it. The whole concept was to help people better understand what was happening to me and I hoped my friends and family might watch.

A few hours later, I went onto my YouTube channel to see if the video had gotten any views. I wasn't looking for my video to go viral. I had not set my expectations too high or too low. I was keeping an open mind when I pulled up the video to check it. I was shocked! It had gotten over 800 views. Considering I was just aiming for friends and family to see it, I was extremely happy that so many people had watched it. Here's the best part—I was completely moved by the incredibly kind and comforting comments made by the viewers. Many people were watching AND taking the time to comment. It was an amazing experience to realize that even strangers cared enough to reach out to me. Reading their encouraging words lifted me up and I started to believe I could have a positive eighth-grade year ending with my graduation and then a happy next move to high school. This would be a dream come true for me. Being happy and successful was all I wanted. I hoped I was getting there.

My Brain XP Friends:
"May 13th" is about a specific incident that happened on May 13, 2014. I was experiencing psychotic symptoms that led me to run away after school. I was found and brought home safely hours later. I wrote this song as a reflection of that day to always keep me aware of how blessed I am to be alive, to be doing so well, and to have family and friends who love me.

Christine XP

Thoughts?

Check out the Brain XP website for my current blog,
music, videos & performances

www.brainxpproject.com

Spare Heart

Pull me in lure me
I won't do this again
all the time you treated me
like I was just a sin
but you should know
I don't care anymore
all those times you were mistaken
and you shut my face to the door
while I was painfully screaming

Get me out of this mess
Get me out of this mess
God, I need some rest oh oh oh

I need a spare heart
mine was taken
it was torn apart
crack crack crack
shattered
it doesn't matter
it doesn't matter
just give me a spare heart
I need a spare heart
just give me a spare heart
I need a spare heart

Pull me in pull me out
break me up break me down
scared to do anything
because of how things have been
but you should know
I'm not scared anymore

Chapter Seven

Spare Heart

My first day of eighth grade finally came. I admit I was nervous. There was a new principal at the school. There was a new pastor at the church. My eighth-grade teacher was also new.

I met the principal and my teacher during a meeting with my therapy counselors and mom over the summer. They seemed very nice. My mom and counselors explained everything I had gone through during seventh grade. They said they understood and were on board with offering support whenever I needed it. They sounded cooperative and I thought everything would be okay.

On that first day, I felt extremely anxious because I was around so many people. The first day of school is exciting, but always a little scary too. The day started with an assembly and the whole school was there. I didn't know there was going to be an assembly, so I grew more anxious. I could feel the buildup starting already. I made it through the assembly, but my body was shaking by the end of it. Sometimes when I get anxious, I start to feel jittery and my teeth chatter. I'm not physically hurt or anything. I just need to calm myself down.

My class and I walked back to our classroom. It was just a couple of hours until the first recess. From the time I stepped into the classroom until the bell rang for recess, I was struggling. It probably didn't look like I was struggling, but inside I was a mess. I was not ready yet to go out into the big crowd—the whole school—for recess. Being in a large crowd, even of my classmates was still very hard for me. As I stood there holding my backpack and wanting to overcome my fear, I was on the verge of tears. I asked myself, "Can I make it outside or not?" I felt frozen.

What I was experiencing that day was so intense. I was only thirteen and I felt terrified in my own schoolyard. Even today, telling the story takes me right back there—as if I am in-the-moment. Try to envision what is happening to me as you read the "real-time" account of this episode of psychosis.

―――――――――――――

I keep standing still, not moving. I am shaking with fear. Finally, I make myself step out of the classroom and try to act like everybody else. I walk about ten feet. I see the demon! I am devastated! What is happening? I see a flash of the happy, new school year I am hoping for. It is instantly gone! Nothing has changed! Rapid thoughts run through my mind. "This is my first day," "I'm back on square one," "How can this be happening?"

I reach out to grab one of my friends by the arm. She is looking in my face. Is she afraid of me? I think, "Please help me!" But I can't say anything! I want to shout, "Something is wrong!" But nothing comes out. I am so afraid. She can't help. She can't see. She doesn't know. Do I look scary to her? All of these kids and teachers are around me and I don't know what to do. Someone, please help me get away from the demon! I am frozen. My body will not move.

I watch my new eighth-grade teacher walk out to the recess area. I look at her. I see her, but I don't believe it is really her. I see the rest of the students, too. They look like regular people, but I don't believe they are real. The demons have taken over everybody! I scream a silent scream, "Every-one around me is a demon!"

I stand here alone, looking around and taking in all the demons—they are my teacher and all the kids. Part of my brain can tell these are people I go to school with, but another part KNOWS I am being tricked by demons, and they want to hurt my friends. Am I crying now? I feel scared and helpless! My heart is pounding, and I think I am panicking, but I can't move from this spot.

I keep standing perfectly still and am gripped with fear. I think I see my mom coming toward me. No! It is two demons, my mom and my teacher. They are watching me and walk closer and closer to me. I see two demons. It cannot be my mom and teacher. I hear the recess bell ring.

I am not outside any more. This place looks like the parish hall. How did I get here? The demon who took over my mom is here, too. Another silent scream, "Where is my mom!"

It is better in the parish hall. I don't feel so confused

now. The rest of the demons are gone. I don't know where they went, but they are not in the parish hall.

One demon is standing very close to me. I am staring at her. I am looking right at her face. I am looking right in her eyes. It is a demon! Where is my mom! What did you do to her?

———————————

Were you able to envision what was happening to me physically, mentally, and emotionally? Telling you about this episode is very difficult and brings back awful memories for me. But it is important to me to help you understand that psychosis creates its own dangerous reality in a person's brain. This is one episode, which I had on the first day of school in the eighth grade when I was thirteen years old.

What happened next is still confusing to me and my memory is not totally clear. While we were still in the parish hall, my mom and I had a conversation. I don't remember what it was about, but I do remember that we talked. I reluctantly walked with the demon (my mom) to the school office. I remember that I was crying. While we were in the office, I overheard the demon talking to someone on the phone. I sat in a chair in the corner of the room and kept crying.

Suddenly, the demon sounded really serious. I started paying closer attention to the conversation. The demon mentioned something about calling an ambulance. It was right in that moment that I snapped out of it. When I overheard the word "ambulance," it scared the hell out of me! That word brought me back to reality. I immediately became aware that all of the last few minutes were not real, that my thinking had been terribly off. I now know that a person likely will not remember the details of what happened in a psychotic episode. They may even argue that something did not happen as others tell about the event. I think it is a kind of black out.

When I say, "I snapped out of it," I literally mean my mom was my mom again. I looked around and I was able to understand people for people. No demons were walking around. I felt such extraordinary joy! What a blessing! Reality had come back to me. The loss of total or partial memory is one strange aspect of psychosis. An unusual outcome may be the sudden clearing of a person's thinking. Why did the word "ambulance" bring me back to reality? I do not know. The truth is that the person experiencing the episode is not in charge of starting or stopping psychosis.

The whole episode lasted about forty-five minutes. It felt so real in the moment. I still don't understand why it happened or why it took so long for me to come back to reality.

Over the next two months, I continued to struggle. I was working really hard with my counselors every week on coping skills and trying different medicines to manage each day. Some days were not bad. On many school days, I could make it through the entire day if I just had a break or two in the school office when I started feeling anxious. Then I could get right back to class. But I was still hearing the demons' voices. When the demons threatened, I always felt my options were limited—especially when I was at school. If the demons ordered me to run away and threatened to hurt the younger children if I didn't, I felt like I had to run away to keep the kids safe. I knew running away was not a good idea, but I also knew allowing a bunch of five-year-old kids to get hurt definitely was bad. The demons' threats made me feel like my life was falling apart.

As I walked toward my classroom at the end of recess one afternoon, I started hearing the demons threatening the students again. I stopped, but then a sudden jerk of compulsion forced me to run. I ran straight through the parish hall and out the doors to the main street. I ran to the nearest neighborhood where I came to a dead end. I stood in the middle of the street. I felt defeated.

Out of nowhere, I heard someone calling my name. I turned around and saw my teacher from seventh grade standing several yards behind me. I didn't even realize that he had come running after me from the school.

I slowly walked over to him. I was expecting him to ask me a lot of questions. "Why did you run off? Where were you going?"

But he didn't ask me anything. He just slowly walked me back to school. When we got back, the principal immediately scolded me. I wasn't surprised, but it stung. Nobody understood the role I was given by the voices. I had to choose between putting myself at risk versus putting kindergartners at risk. In my head, I did the right thing. It was a courageous, brave thing to protect children from harm, but obeying the demon voices always ended in a bad outcome. Still, how could I not play the role the voices demanded? It was worth the risk to me.

The school called my mom to come pick me up. I went home that day with the most horrible feeling inside. I was not going to get much help from the school. They simply didn't understand.

I continued to go to school every day and tried my best to do well. I am not a quitter. I felt like I had to defeat the demons and the only way to do that was by succeeding despite their efforts to make me fail.

I LOVED my school and I had been going there for ten years. I decided that graduating and moving on from the school would be the ultimate retaliation against the demons.

I knew my goal and believed I was capable of accomplishing it. I knew I could make it through this last year at my school and then move on to high school. In that moment, I felt confident in myself. I was still not very happy, but I was hopeful.

Days passed, and I was not getting much better. I was not getting worse, but progress was at a standstill. My treatment team at the psychosis prevention center was in the process of figuring out my diagnosis and still experimenting with different medications and dosages. Plus, my mom brought me to see a new psychiatrist as well. I learned that my diagnosis is bipolar disorder. I was put on a new medication that is known to help many people with my diagnosis. I knew medications take time to start having a real effect, but not everybody in the world understood that.

On November 5, 2014, I crossed the street after school. The demons were in my head again tempting me. Claiming they would leave me alone if I got away. I will admit I was struggling. I knew my mind was a little off, but I also knew that my sanity—my ability to think—was still present. I was not crazy. I was not insane. I was just confused, and I thought I might be able to trick the demons by walking across the street after school and coming back in a few minutes.

When I crossed the street, I headed over to the recreation center. One of the safety patrol students saw me and notified the principal. Keep in mind, my school was very small—everyone knew everyone and everything that happened there. Another student walking across the street after school would not have caught a second glance. Not me. My seventh-grade teacher and the principal came over to me and they walked back to school with me.

My parents were called by the school to come pick me up. When they arrived, they immediately were taken to the principal's office. I didn't even know they were at the school.

I was waiting in a separate office for my parents thinking they were on their way to pick me up when I learned they were in a meeting with the principal. I waited and waited and waited. I felt confused and the whole situation seemed very strange to me.

Finally, my parents came out of the principal's office and I assumed we were leaving to go home. I stood up to go, but when I looked at my mom I saw tears streaming down her face. I asked her, "Why are you crying?" as we started walking to the car. I insisted that she tell me, so she did. She told me, "You are no longer allowed to go to school here."

My initial thought was that some sort of arrangement was being worked out for me to have some time off to do work from home or something like that. When my mom said that there was no arrangement, I dropped my bags and just stared at her.

Full panic mode took over. I had no control of the rush of feelings and thoughts that were flooding me. I started crying. I didn't understand. I felt devastated. I knew other kids who had ditched school before, so why was I different? Those kids didn't get expelled. All my actions came from a good heart. I knew I was having problems, but couldn't they work out some type of temporary solution for me. I just needed a little more time for the new medication to kick in.

I started screaming and both my seventh and eighth-grade teachers came over. I was hysterical. Everything felt shattered. I couldn't think. All my friends were at this school. I didn't even know anyone else. I had been here since I was three years old. I couldn't imagine that I would have to change schools and figure out my life all over again with no one I knew around me.

My teachers came over to where we were standing, but there was nothing they could do. They had no power over the principal, and apparently, neither did my family.

I walked to the car with my mom. I cried for hours after we got home. Eventually, I tried to get myself together, so that I could make two phone calls. I called my two best friends to let them know that I had been removed from the school. I thought they would be able to explain what had happened to the rest of my class. The problem was that no one understood what was happening, so no one ever said anything. It was as if nothing had happened. I simply was not at school anymore. No one reached out, but I don't blame them. They had no clue how hurt I was by the school's decision. I wish they could have understood what was happening to me because of the bipolar disorder diagnosis. Maybe then they would have been able to help. I may sound selfish for saying that, but what I needed was help. I just needed help and a little patience.

A couple weeks later, we received a letter from the principal confirming my permanent disenrollment from school. In addition, it stated I could not attend any of the eighth-grade graduation functions I had been looking forward to for the last ten years with my friends. I could not stop thinking about the kids I knew who had ditched school and had received little or no consequence or punishment as a result. All I did was walk across the street after school was out. Life truly isn't fair.

My Brain XP Friends:
"Spare Heart" guides you through all the times that people treat you badly or do wrongful things to you. After being kicked out of my school, I was so incredibly depressed that living life became more and more difficult for me. I wrote my song, "Spare Heart," to release those feelings of sadness, hurt, and anger and in doing so, I truly began to see that living life is the greatest blessing I have. No one, including myself, will take that from me.
How do you cope with feelings like this?
Do you have a way that is positive and strenthening for you?

Christine XP

Thoughts?

Check out the Brain XP website for my current blog,
music, videos & performances

www.brainxpproject.com

Shy

I don't know what we got right here
but I can tell that it's crystal clear
I am shy
and I know I may not make sense
but you know that I won't pretend
I'm just shy

Would you give me a chance
I haven't gotten one yet

Don't blow me off 'cuz I'm shy
Don't rough me up 'cuz I, I am not that kind
And don't you tell me I'm not your type
I know you like me I, I can read your eyes
I'm shy I'm shy I'm shy
I hope you don't change your mind

I don't know what we got right here
but you can tell as I'm whispering
I am shy
and I know it may not seem like I like you
but that's just 'cuz I am shy

Chapter Eight

Shy

One of the most difficult challenges I have always had is adapting to new situations. Change is hard for me. Because I could no longer attend my former school, I had to adjust to a different one. We had very few options when it came to choosing a new school for me. I ended up transferring from my small private school to a large local public middle school.

I knew no one. I didn't know my way around campus. The school schedule and hours were new to me. I had never used a locker before. Most difficult of all, I was still deeply depressed.

I spent a lot of my time figuring out where to go and what to do. I was at my highest level of anxiety since before I started having hallucinations. I was far from being a "great fit" in my new school.

I entered the school in the middle of eighth grade, so everybody had already formed their groups of friends. I couldn't figure out how to squeeze into one of those groups.

After a few months of struggles, I finally started to get the hang of things. My school counselor was incredibly kind and looked out for me. She helped me get through so many difficult moments!

Because of my diagnoses of depression and bipolar disorder and my struggles at my previous school, I qualified for special education services. The school assigned a case manager to me when the school district psychologist determined that I needed extra support. My case manager along with other clinicians assessed me for an

Individual Education Plan (IEP). The IEP allowed me to have specific accommodations based on how I learn. Once the document was finalized, my teachers provided those accommodations to me in my classes. The purpose of an IEP is to help a student who has a condition that interferes with his or her success in school. The accommodations I needed were simple—a little extra time on certain tasks, breaks if I was feeling overwhelmed, and occasional counseling appointments. It seemed like it took forever to get my IEP, but it was incredibly helpful from the first day it was put in place. It was worth the wait.

I started having lunch in my case manager's classroom and I ended up meeting a few girls there that were super kind and welcoming. I never grew close to any of them, but it was nice to know I could go somewhere for lunch and not be alone.

I finished out my eighth-grade year. It was not easy. There were many tears and sad days. I must have broken down and cried about a hundred times, but I was able to overcome with the support I received. The change and adjustment to the new school was very difficult but I truly believe I proved the leaders of my old school wrong to have dismissed me. I woke up every day and pushed myself to attend classes and make it through each day just as I had at my previous school. When I began receiving the consistent help I needed at school, I showed I was still the good student who wanted and was able to learn and be successful at school. My ability, drive, and positive attitude had not disappeared because I experienced symptoms of psychosis. With therapy, medication, family support, and IEP help at school I began to recover my mental and emotional stability.

I ended eighth grade on a good note. I wouldn't say I was happy, but there were more smiles peeking through on my face. That told me I was heading in the right direction.

I was still being prescribed certain medications and I was still hoping they would have a positive effect on my overall mood. Happiness was all I wanted, and I was getting there.

My Brain XP Friends:
"Shy" lets you know that you should not change for anybody unless you feel it is a positive change. If you are naturally shy or have moments of shyness, that is absolutely fine. Be understanding that everybody has a story that can affect the attributes of any person.

Christine XP

Thoughts?

Check out the Brain XP website for my current blog,
music, videos & performances

www.brainxpproject.com

Okay

Side by side
with our brothers we'd pick some pretty good fights
you and I
after school on those Friday nights
Side by side
and you know I
would take away all those silly words I'd say
at year five

Things are not the same
We are what you need
we go ten years deep
I wanna' do more than pray
I just wanna' make you okay
Okay

Side by side
all of those laughs and really good cries
I could not
no, I could not describe
Side by side
every time
I wish you were here
then I'd disappear in my own mind

I would drown in the ocean water
I can't swim in water that's 10 years deep but for you
I would do what I have to cry and laugh to
be around you

Okay

Chapter Nine

Okay

Middle school had been a nightmare and going into high school was definitely scary. I kept telling myself that high school couldn't be worse than the past three years.

My first day of ninth grade went pretty well. I was terrified I would not be able to find my way around the large campus. I didn't have any friends that I was looking forward to seeing, which made me feel like a complete loser standing around with no idea where to go or what to do.

I pushed through. I carefully walked to each class, checking every single door to make sure I was at the right room number. I tried to socialize to the best of my ability and I honestly thought that I might have started to look normal.

Of course, then there were the locker rooms to figure out. No matter how hard I tried, my anxiety got the best of me every time I walked inside. I could barely get my locker open because my hands shook so much. I couldn't dial the right numbers.

Lunch was horrible too. I sat at a small table in the corner of a courtyard at the school. I sat alone with nothing to do, so I pulled out my phone and pretended to play a game on it. I was too scared to even turn my phone on because I didn't want to forget to turn it back off when the bell rang for class.

Anxiety still was my biggest problem. It cut me off from being able to make friends or feel confident about learning the routine of high school.

Gradually, I started to fit in a little bit better. After a few months, I found a really nice classroom to eat lunch in. I made a few friends who also hung out there. Things seemed to be coming together. I told myself to be patient.

I worked my butt off to get good grades and to excel academically. I ended the school year with several ninth-grade awards. I was the best writer in the ninth grade. I had the highest GPA in the ninth grade and I was also selected as most likely to be the class valedictorian.

It felt good to see my hard work pay off, but I knew I wasn't truly happy inside. Something was blocking me from being able to enjoy these awards—awards that anyone else would think of as amazing accomplishments. With summer on the way, I had an opportunity to refresh and reboot. I needed a good summer break to help me bounce back with confidence and hope.

Summer was wonderful. One of my very good friends had moved out of state a few years earlier. She flew out to California for the early summer and we had so much fun. She stayed with a relative who lived close to me. My friend came for a few weeks and it was seriously the best summer I had ever had.

We hung out almost every day. Our bond was already pretty strong, but we grew even closer. She's one of the few people I feel comfortable calling a best friend.

The whole summer was a blast, but it was sad when it ended. I literally cried for three days after my friend left to go back home. I also had to face the fact that I had to go back to school, even though I dreaded it. It felt like I had barely made it through my freshman year.

Why should I continue to spend time every day in a place where I felt painfully uncomfortable and unwelcome? It made no sense to me.

Sophomore year came anyway! I did my very best to attend school daily and look like I was completely engaged in learning. But that is not how I felt. I sat in class and acted as if I was listening to the words coming out of the teacher's mouth, while actually I was taking in little or no information.

I began to really struggle. I was so unhappy, and my depression was creeping up. I hated school. I think I hated it so much because I didn't have any close friends. I had acquaintances, but I had no friends I could really talk to. This struggle turned into a huge setback.

First, I began crying during lunch. Then I began crying during class. I felt invisible. It was like nobody even saw me or knew who I was. It was not a situation I wanted to be in. I was unhappy, and no one wants to be unhappy. I just kept going the best I could. This was my sophomore year and the support structure I had in eighth grade was not in place here at high school. There was no place I could go when I was feeling overwhelmed to calm down and the school counselor was only on campus a couple days a week. Eventually, the school administration began sending me home. My parents called for a special IEP meeting to amend my plan to get some temporary resources in place to help me out. We were advised that the financial resources available to my school were not adequate enough for my needs. My parents and I made the tough decision to switch schools once again.

Six weeks after the start of my new school year, I left the big public high school to go to a very small independent study charter school. It was extremely different from any school I had ever attended. At this point I had been to a small private school, two large public schools, and now a tiny independent study charter school. This is

115

where I plan to graduate high school and I am so grateful I have this opportunity.

The independent study philosophy sounds exactly like what it is. I learned to study on my own and teach myself the material. I do the work. I turn it in. It's pretty simple. I study one class at a time. Each class is completed in four weeks. It takes a lot of self-discipline. The thing that has been so helpful for me is the flexible schedule. I go into the classroom a few days a week and the rest I do from home.

This was a huge change. I have never been so happy with a change in my life. I immediately began to succeed mentally, emotionally, and academically at the new charter school.

Along with the positive changes happening following the switch in schools during the tenth grade, I finally graduated from the psychosis prevention center's program. It took thirty months of hard work and progressive treatment from age twelve to fifteen, but I finally reached a point of stability. I haven't had a significant hallucination experience in three years. I no longer experience extended periods of depression. I confess I do battle anxiety every day, but I have learned how to manage it, so I am not missing life. I can function and take care of myself and simply no longer need the extended services. I do see my psychiatrist once a month and love to go to therapy each week—usually to let my therapist know how great I am doing!

I graduated from the program with the biggest smile, feeling happiness spread over and through me like bright, warm sunshine. I felt the confident energy I knew I needed to move forward with my life. I have developed good coping skills and am attending a school that is a "good fit" for me. I am taking control of my own life again.I need one more aspect added to my life, socialization. At an independent study school, it is hard to create friendships, but not impossible. This is my next challenge to overcome!

In the meantime, I have strengthened my relationship with God. I haven't lost my straight "A" track record at school. Writing and my music continue to be my constant companions and my best way to escape from stress and find a larger purpose. I am becoming the person I want to be. I am reaching out to other teenagers who are experiencing similar challenges and seeing if I can help them find HOPE.

I have strengthened my
relationship with God.

—Christine XP

My Brain XP Friends:
"Okay" was written as an outreach of
comfort for my best friend who moved
to another state. Her friends were gone,
and life gradually became very tough
for her. I could completely relate to how
she was feeling, so I wrote this for her.
I hope you can relate to it as well.
Have you been encouraged or given
encouragement to a friend?

Christine XP

Thoughts?

Check out the Brain XP website for my current blog,
music, videos & performances

www.brainxpproject.com

Stop Hiding

Lonely
all alone
but I'm not on my own
I see things people just don't see
but I crave to be
who I want to be

It's a long long road ahead
So I picked myself up and started again instead
and unlike all the other books I have read
this winding twisted road has no end

But it's a privilege
to be like this
understanding what most of the world will never know
so stop hiding
and let it show
so stop hiding
and let people know

Isolated and anxious
no words to describe this feeling
I am speechless
I want to be like everybody else
but I would much rather stay true to myself

Chapter Ten

Stop Hiding

As I moved through the rest of tenth grade and began eleventh grade, I saw that I was improving mentally and emotionally. I still had bad days. I still cried. I still became moody. I worked diligently to get to the more stable place where I am now at age sixteen, in my junior year of high school. It wasn't easy, though. One of the differences in me at age twelve and now at sixteen is that I learned from my various therapies to identify my triggers and how to use coping skills. That was something I had not been very good at before. I know my triggers. My top triggers are anything NEW (people, locations, situations), large groups of people, making presentations, unfamiliar or loud noises, flames, and people in conflict. Since I know my triggers, I try to avoid them when I can. And when I can't, I use my coping skills.

It's important to find the right coping skills that will work for you. They are different for each person. As I have said several times already, writing and making music are, by far, my top coping skills. I lock myself away for a few hours and let my mind wander after school. It helps me relax and get out my feelings on paper in words and song. Another coping skill that I have become very adept at is "planning." I plan everything! Planning helps me be prepared for what will happen during the day. This is particularly helpful if something new pops up. For example, I just recently went to see Halsey in concert. Normally, a concert venue would create a lot of anxiety for me. I called my cousin to ask him to come with me. We planned out where we would park and how far the walk was to the arena. We planned what time we would leave to make sure we got there in plenty of time, and then we planned to leave even a little earlier, so the crowd would be less hectic. We planned to buy Halsey merchandise before the show started so the lines would be shorter. And we stayed after the concert was over, so the crowds would thin out. I know it sounds very un-spontaneous and that is correct. But I had the best time ever and never got anxious the whole night! Other great coping skills are deep breathing, fidget toys to keep my hands occupied, talking to a friend, exercise, getting lots of sleep, journaling, dance, listening to music, playing with my dog Sparky, and distracting myself from whatever is making me anxious. Because I've learned how to cope better, my difficulties don't come up as much. It is a win-win situation. Better coping. Fewer difficulties.

I've had a dream since I was a little kid. I've always wanted to make a positive difference in the world. I didn't know how I was going to do it. I wasn't sure if I was going to impact one person or thousands of people. I just knew I wanted to leave a good mark on the world. But when I started struggling with depression and psychosis, I lost a lot of the motivation to work toward my dream.

After I switched to the independent study school, my life took off again. I was heading in a great direction. I sat down and told myself that having self-discipline is necessary at this school. I have to work hard and stay focused to keep myself on track. I will admit I procrastinate at times, but I know how to push myself to get my work done.

My dream is what drives me, even though it may not be clear yet. One day my dream is to sell a hundred copies of one of my songs. The next day my dream is to perform one of my songs in front of a thousand people. I know one thing for certain about my dream. It will always include making a positive impact in this world.

The best part about having this dream is that I have already glimpsed how special it is. During a family gathering at my house, my aunt looked at me and said, "Christine, you have touched so many hearts with your music and story!" Another time, a friend called me and told me that the reason she is so close to God is because of me and my determination to get well and be the person God wants me to be. Seeing and hearing people share these things with me has been such an amazing experience. Seeing my dream through the eyes of others, like my aunt and friend, gives me hope knowing there will always be more for me to do.

With my dream as my focus, I started planning. I already knew I loved music. I could create songs at my house with no problems. It was then that I realized all the songs I had written were products of the many feelings I experienced as I learned to live with a mental disorder. Music was vital to the plan I was creating.

Since my writing skills were pretty decent, I figured I could try writing about my life in a real book format. There certainly was plenty to write about! I just needed to set a goal and stick with it. I have had a tough time reading books for a while now (my mind gets distracted easily), so I thought writing one probably would not be easy. I still put this idea into the plan. It might be important later, so I didn't want to throw the idea away.

After a few more additions to my masterpiece plan, I stopped planning and started working on it. My plan was to pull the music and the writing together as a way to share my story about mental illness.

As I worked on writing my book and creating a few songs, my ideas started flooding out. When I was struggling, I couldn't find *anything* about mental illness from a teenager's point of view—no books, videos, or songs. I think that needs to change and someone needs to do something. I want to be that person. I want to make more YouTube videos on teen mental health and I want to set up my own website as a space to land when searching for information on teenage mental health. That is my focus and it quickly has become my passion.

Advocacy has always been a part of me, but it came to life when I started working on this project. With ten of my mental health inspired songs ready to be recorded and an incredibly personal book that I am about to finish in the next paragraph, I can firmly say I am the happiest I have ever been.

I am Christine XP and my journey as the founder of the Brain XP Community has only just begun. Being a member of such an inclusive community means so much to me. Please know you are always welcome. The road to a happy, healthy life starts with understanding. This journey of understanding will lead us to the elimination of the words mental "illness." Join me!

I've had a dream since I was a little kid. I've always wanted to make a positive difference in the world.

—Christine XP

My Brain XP Friends:
"Stop Hiding" spreads the message
that we are proud to be who we are.
There is no need to hide from the
world. Let people know who you are
instead. We have bright spirits within
us, and we will not hide because
we are Brain XP!

Christine XP

Thoughts?

Check out the Brain XP website for my current blog,
music, videos & performances

www.brainxpproject.com

Three Perspectives

A Glimpse Behind the Mask

My Mom's Perspective

Mom XP

"Your daughter has a serious mental disorder." Seven words I never imagined hearing. Seven words that have changed our lives forever.

I had always considered myself a pretty decent mom. I was nothing if not organized and structured. Before my first child was born, I read all 600 pages of *What to Expect When You're Expecting* from cover to cover! I wanted to learn everything I could to be a good mom. Like many working moms, I decided shortly after Christine was born that I wanted to be at home more with my two young children. I resigned a much-loved career position in advertising, joined my husband's business, and leveraged my free time to do volunteer work at my kids' school in order to be more involved in their lives. My husband and I spent ALL our evenings and weekends with the kids. We had annual passes to Legoland and used them every month; we played games together in the living room most evenings; we made up sports activities down at the local field; and went to church each week. We went to every school activity—ice cream socials, soccer, football and basketball games, holiday get-togethers, carnivals—you name it, we were there. We set up our house rules very early on. The kids always knew faith, family, and school were their priorities. They learned strong study habits and excelled at school. Were they ever mischievous? Of course! But they were perfectly healthy, bright, humorous, normal kids. At bedtime, we would ask them, "What did you do today to be the best you could be?" We always got the greatest answers that showed their positive self-esteem and inner strength.

I remember someone telling me when my children were toddlers, "Treasure these years before they grow older and the problems begin." I can honestly say we have enjoyed our children more every year they have grown from cuddly toddlers to independent teenagers and every year has been a little more special than the last. They are truly wonderful children and we are blessed, but we were not naive enough to think their journey would be trouble free. We were prepared to handle poor academics, negative behavior at school, potential drug use, and even the possibility of an unexpected pregnancy. We thought we had all our bases covered, but we were wrong.

Christine would be considered the quintessential "ideal" child. She had always been a straight "A" student, had tons of friends, had lots of energy, loved to play all team sports, had an engaging sense of humor, participated in school programs outside academics, did volunteer work, and communicated well with everyone from friends to younger children to adults. We found it cute that Christine had a couple quirky personality traits from early on as a toddler. She was a stickler for cleanliness. She not only made sure she washed her hands before every meal, but she also checked to make sure everyone else did too. She was adamant about not eating off anyone else's plate. If anyone asked to taste something from her plate, she would carefully cut a portion off to the side. The result of her discipline was that she was always healthy. She rarely caught a cold, much less the flu. Over time, we did become aware that having control was important to Christine. We never considered this something to be concerned about. In fact, quite the opposite, we admired it as a strong personality trait.

We recognized the possibility that the need for control had become a larger issue as sixth-grade camp came into view. In the year leading up to sixth-grade camp, we did realize Christine was struggling with going to sleepovers at a friend's house. She always wanted to go to them, but invariably I would get the midnight phone call that

Christine was not feeling well. Then, as soon as she got into the car to come home, her stomachache seemed to fade. I never doubted she actually had those tummy aches. You could see the sense of being overwhelmed on her face when I would pick her up to come home. Her tense expression would slowly subside as we got closer to home. Her dad and I needed a little extra help with this one. It took some long hand-holding sessions, but we were able to convince Christine to try counseling for this one issue. She was so afraid someone would find out and that her friends might make fun of her. I promised her we would keep it to ourselves just in the family, so she agreed. It took a couple sessions for Christine to get comfortable, but she made great strides with her counselor in a very short time. Her therapist was a young intern finalizing his education at a local university. He made her feel comfortable and he fit our financial budget as well. In less than six months, Christine had conquered her fear, gained valuable insight, and learned some valuable coping skills for the future.

When Christine was twelve years old entering seventh grade, her older brother graduated their elementary school and headed off to high school. This left Christine to enter the middle school years of her education at the school she and her brother had attended together for the previous ten years. About this time, Christine broke her ankle for the third time in three years. This injury coincided with a change in coaching staff and philosophy of her soccer franchise. My husband and I decided to remove Christine from that franchise until her ankle could fully heal. We noticed something was not quite right with our daughter. We assumed Christine might be missing her brother, although, I doubt they ever said two words to each other all day long at school since both had their own circle of friends. We thought she might miss the sense of comfort that came from having her brother at school. Perhaps, she just needed a little transition time. We also thought Christine was feeling lonely with her two good friends remaining on the soccer team without her. We figured these were normal pre-teen adjustments

135

that she would learn to handle with time.

Over the next few months, Christine taught herself to play guitar and spent a lot of time in her room playing music. A couple of months later, she began taking piano lessons and writing song lyrics as well. Christine has always been creative, especially in the use of the English language. Her dad and I thought this was a good indication that Christine had found a new niche in her life. But, at the same time, we realized Christine was not participating in other activities. She stopped hanging out with her brother or us after dinner when we watched our favorite TV shows. She came up with excuses for why she did not want to play games together. She also stopped participating in school activities. We were unaware that she had dropped out of the school chorus and the student council. It took us another couple of months before we understood something very dangerous was happening. By now, it was close to the end of the first semester and it became very clear to us as parents that Christine was isolating herself—from EVERYTHING and EVERYONE.

Shortly after Christmas break of Christine's seventh-grade year, we received a phone call from her teacher who asked us to come to school for a meeting. Her teacher and school principal were both at this meeting. They explained that Christine had been crying at school and looked very unhappy. They also mentioned Christine was avoiding eye contact and had stopped raising her hand in class to answer questions. We reviewed some of Christine's assignments. Her handwriting had changed and was now minuscule, so tiny it was difficult to read. I suddenly thought her tiny handwriting looked to me like Christine was trying to be tiny too, as if she were in hiding. This was not the Christine her teacher and principal had come to know over the past nine years. They were genuinely worried. At this point, our small concern that Christine was just having a rough transition into her teenage years became a much larger concern. But, we were not even close to understanding what was really happening to our child.

After more convincing, Christine started going to counseling again in February, shortly after our school conference. The several weeks that followed were fast and chaotic. Each week brought a new symptom, of just what, we did not understand. Christine began to self-harm by cutting her wrists. She was not suicidal. She never cut herself deeply enough to cause serious physical damage, but it was obvious she wanted the pain inside her to just stop. I remember her telling me, "Mom, I'm scared. I don't know what's wrong with me." It broke my heart to hear her say this and to realize not only could I not fix what was wrong *for* her, I did not know what was wrong *with* her!

One month later, in March, Christine admitted to seeing and hearing things that were not there. Thinking back through the Christmas holiday and the new year, I am now confident Christine had started to see and hear things for a few months before admitting it to us, or even to herself. Even now, it's painful to think about how incredibly afraid and alone she must have felt. And I was right there and could not see it! Once she admitted to hallucinating, the flood gates opened, and she began hallucinating all the time. She heard "demons" in her mind which told her she was a bad person. We began referring to them as "the guys." They would threaten to harm her brother, her teacher, or her friends. There were times I would have to call and talk to my son or her teacher to convince Christine they were okay and not in any danger. Christine would be genuinely panicked about their safety until I had done so. The phone calls would help her calm down and stop worrying that "the guys" had followed through on their threats. Christine may have intellectually understood that she was hallucinating, and the demons were not real, but at the time she experienced them, they were ABSOLUTELY REAL to her in that moment. As the hallucinations increased and became more intense, Christine almost completely stopped talking to her dad and brother, further isolating herself.

On the other hand, she needed me to be with her all the time. It was like she became a small child again due to the overwhelming fears in the world inside her head where she was living. Upon hearing Christine's admissions of hallucinations, her therapist referred us to a comprehensive Psychosis Prevention and Early Intervention Program.

On April 24, 2014, Christine and I met with the therapist from the early intervention program. I walked him through the last six months of Christine's emotional volcanic journey. Christine refers to her emotional ups and downs like lava in an active volcano—never quite knowing when it will erupt. The therapist simply looked at me in a completely calm manner and said, *"You are going to want to fix this, but you can't."* It's like he read my mind! Later I thought, "I'll bet every parent who walks through the therapist's door is thinking the exact same thing, 'Please help me fix this!'" Over the next few minutes, I came to understand Christine would be taking a very long journey with a heavy weight to bear. I also came to realize that with time, patience, and several life adjustments in our family and environment, we could help Christine learn to control her symptoms. We felt like we had found hope; but then three weeks later May 13th came along.

On May 13, 2014, near the end of the seventh-grade school year, I went to pick up Christine from school. She wasn't there. She was missing. Apparently, Christine decided to make a deal with "the guys." They kept telling her to run away. She did not want to run away, but neither did she want "the guys" bugging her. So, being a clever twelve year old, she figured she would run away after school and "the guys" would vanish, then she would come right back and be done with them! Of course, we didn't know what had happened or where she was. We couldn't reach her by phone and none of her friends had seen her leave school. There were multiple fires throughout the San Diego area that day and it was a very warm 95 degrees. We called the police three times to report Christine as missing but could not receive any help because of the immediate urgency of the fires. After three and a half hours of searching (which seemed like an eternity), my husband found her walking around lost in the military housing near the school. When they arrived home, something had changed in the way Christine was communicating with us. She was talking openly and honestly about every detail of her psychosis-induced adventure. Before this event, getting Christine to talk about her visions and voices had been very difficult. In fact, getting Christine to talk at all was difficult due to her continual isolation. Although there were still many months ahead of us to battle, Christine's openly talking to us without fear was the starting point of her gaining control over her symptoms.

The Early Intervention Program has multiple support programs for helping Christine and other teenagers facing similar challenges— individual therapy, multi-family group therapy for problem solving, school support, occupational therapy, peer counseling, and medication. Christine took advantage of every one of them until we found the programs that worked best for her. By far the most difficult and frustrating part of Christine's journey was and still is medications. There are tremendous medications on the market that can truly improve one's quality of life when facing severe symptoms of psychosis. But the path to discovering the correct medication regimen for an individual is often very long and sometimes excruciatingly long, especially when such severe symptoms appear so early in a child like Christine who was only twelve years old when early onset psychosis set in. The effects of any psychiatric medication can be both exceptionally positive or dreadfully negative depending on numerous factors. Therefore, prescribing any given medication must be done in small incremental doses. It can take weeks and often months before real change is seen in the person's mood or behavior. In addition to the waiting, there are also the side effects of some medications to consider as well—memory loss, nausea, restlessness, drowsiness—it is not fun. After the incident of May 13th, Christine started the first of many regimens of different medications and adjustments in dosages.

The consensus of the treatment team for Christine's diagnosis at that time was Depression with Psychotic Features. We learned not to give too much weight to any given diagnosis. There is a lot of overlap amongst symptoms of various psychological disorders and it is not unusual for diagnoses to change. Over time, Christine showed increasing signs of gaining control. Therapy was a huge plus for Christine. She took to heart everything she learned in these sessions and diligently implemented new coping skills and other helpful strategies. She put together weekly plans for how to handle different stressful situations she might encounter. She learned that stress is often the instigator of psychosis. She was absolutely determined not to be defeated. We were feeling hopeful again; then came the end of summer and the return to school.

Just before the eighth-grade school year began, Christine was back-sliding into more depressive symptoms. She began to self-injure again, cutting her arms. "The guys" were telling her to hurt herself in different ways. She came to me on a Thursday afternoon a week before school started and told me, "Mom, I think you need to take me to the hospital. I don't think I can control myself from not hurting myself again." Even through all the hallucinations, Christine had the insight and understanding to ask for help. We went to Children's Hospital, both of us thinking they would likely recommend Christine stay for a day or two. I had told Christine that I would be able to stay with her, since I knew all the hospital beds at Children's Hospital had a daybed next to them for the parents. Wow, were we wrong—again!

Christine was admitted into Children and Adolescent Psychiatric Services (CAPS), what she now politely calls "prison." Christine refers to CAPS as a prison because the facility looks cold and sterile.

There were no pencils, pens, or anything that could possibly be considered a potential weapon. The toilets were metal. The kids were not allowed any music or iPods. Christine HATED that. We could only visit for one hour a day in the early evening. The purpose of CAPS is to evaluate teenagers to help ensure they would not self-harm following discharge. When we were told to go home rather than stay with Christine, she looked at me with tears running down her cheeks screaming, "How can you leave me here!" The moment we left, I desperately wanted to go back and bring her home. Christine was allowed to call home and talk for a few minutes a couple times a day. She would call each time in tears desperately begging me to bring her home. I knew in my mind that leaving her in the hospital was something we needed to do to ensure her safety in the short term. But I could not get my heart to understand. At one point my husband, son, and I stopped at a sandwich shop to grab lunch on the way to visit Christine when she called me on my cell phone. Again, she was crying and pleading with me to come get her. I was sitting in the corner of this restaurant with tears streaming down my face searching for anything to say that could ease her pain. Her calls, her pleading, and tears from both of us continued like this for five intolerably long days before she was finally released to come home. The most positive outcome from the CAPS experience was when Christine told me, "I never want to go back there again!" She meant that she was ready to double down and start fighting even harder to work her treatment plan. She would indeed learn to fight harder because more trouble was still ahead, but this time not from her disorder. Sadly, the next bout of trouble came from the stigma and ignorance surrounding Christine's diagnosis of a brain disorder.

Eighth grade started the next week. One thing that is commonplace with almost all young people diagnosed with a brain disorder like depression, anxiety, bipolar disorder, or schizophrenia is that change creates anxiety and the more anxiety, the higher the likelihood of an onset of psychosis. Therefore, much of therapy focuses on learning how to cope in changing situations. We prepared by bringing Christine's psychosis prevention program counselors to her school and put together a plan with the administration and her teachers on what to do in the various situations. We had all our ducks in a row and Christine wanted so very much to succeed both in school and with this plan for the school faculty. The one area where she never faltered was school. Christine was absolutely committed to graduating with all her friends despite having to cope with the intermittent symptoms of anxiety, depression, and psychosis. The first day of school was full of anxiety triggers—new administration, new teacher, big school-wide assembly. It was too much happening at one time. Christine was at recess when "the guys" came out in her mind, and she saw them kill her teacher from seventh grade. She was so upset she started yelling at the demons on the playground. All previous psychotic breaks had been reasonably quiet and short-lived. The school immediately called me, and I only lived five minutes away. When I arrived, Christine was still in a state of psychosis and was standing off to the side of the playground by the Parish Hall. I walked over to her and her teacher. The bell rang, and I walked Christine to the office where she sat down in the corner chair. This was the longest psychotic incident (45 minutes) Christine had experienced and it was the ONLY incident I ever witnessed myself. I tried to talk to Christine and let her know her teacher was not dead, that he was fine. I called her medical counselor and asked Christine to talk to her on the phone. When I handed her my phone, Christine wouldn't take it. She accused me of tampering with the phone. She started talking to me like I was one of the demons. She recognized me, but she thought I was being manipulated by the demons. At this point, I was speaking with her counselor about calling an ambulance when Christine snapped out of the incident. She was calm and asked if she could go back to class now, understanding everything that had just happened.

We decided we would supplement Christine's therapies by adding a recognized psychiatrist to her team of support. We received a referral to the Cognitive Assessment and Risk Evaluation Program at the University of California San Diego Medical Center. Christine's psychiatrist evaluated her symptoms of the past year and concluded a different diagnosis than the depression we had been treating. She diagnosed Christine with bipolar disorder. She explained how Christine's symptoms of depression, severe anxiety, restlessness, and psychotic incidents appeared more consistent with this different mood disorder. We had felt for a while that we were missing a piece of Christine's mind puzzle and maybe this was it. The psychiatrist made one significant change to Christine's treatment plan—we changed medications AGAIN. Christine began the slow process of adjustment to lithium. Christine's world of psychosis was very frightening at times, but there were several things we absolutely knew about Christine that made us feel she was safe. One was we knew with certainty she would never harm anyone around her. In fact, it was when the "guys" threatened to hurt people that she did whatever she could think of to protect those people from the "guys" and any potential harm. This is the case for the vast majority of young people with psychosis; they are far more likely to be the victim of harm than to cause harm to another person.

Christine functioned reasonably well at school for the next few weeks. During this whole process of gaining control of her symptoms over the past twelve months, Christine continued to maintain her straight "A" average. She was tracking her activities, emotions, anxiety levels, and the coping skills she was practicing each day. She was attending class and could take breaks when she started to feel overwhelmed. She was making real strides in symptom control, but it was still rocky at times. In late October, "the guys" showed up at recess after a morning of unexpected stressors (substitute teacher, making a class presentation, and her class arriving to mass late resulting in them having to walk in front of the whole church). She described to me that "the guys" appeared more solid than in previous appearances and they were out on the playground amongst her friends. "The guys" threatened to hurt her friends if she did not run away. She became frightened and wanted to protect her friends. She ran out to the front of the school in the hope "the guys" would leave her friends alone. Her teacher from seventh grade saw her leave and ran after her. After several more minutes Christine came out of the psychotic state and her teacher escorted her back to the school grounds. Christine was then given a verbal reprimand from the new administrator for leaving the school campus. The following week, we were called into school. We were told that due to liability issues Christine could no longer attend classes at the school she had attended since she was three years old. This decision was given to us without discussion or input just six months short of Christine's eighth-grade graduation.

Christine was absolutely devastated. She was now not only having to deal with her brain disorder, but also the loss of her support system on top of it. The only friends she had ever known were at that school and she felt completely alone. My husband and I made numerous phone calls and wrote multiple letters just to get ANYONE to talk to us. We finally received communication from the school stating they talk to us. would allow Christine to be home-schooled and were willing to provide the school work for her. The one thing you should NEVER do to a child who is struggling with a brain disorder is ISOLATE them. This was the only time during Christine's entire struggle that I was afraid she might become suicidal. We continued to try to reach anyone to start a dialogue where we could brainstorm alternate solutions to her being permanently withdrawn from this school. Looking back, I see her removal from this school as an overwhelming loss both to Christine and the school itself. All I could think was what an opportunity was lost to teach the other children in the school about mental illness and how the school and church community could have supported one of their fellow students who was in need as Christ would have done. Would a child with a physical illness have received that support?

Christine has not experienced a full psychotic incident since that ten-minute absence from campus that day. The stigma surrounding mental illness is present in all aspects of life where there is fear and ignorance, even in the places we thought were the safest and most comforting for our children and ourselves.

After learning of her school's decision, we enrolled Christine in public school a couple weeks later, just prior to the end of the fall semester. She was depressed and lonely, but the lithium was slowly starting to work. The intensity of her hallucinations was fading. In addition, the school had the most amazing and patient guidance counselor who took the time to give Christine a place to be quiet when she needed it and the understanding she needed to complete her middle school education. We also met with the school district's psychiatrist and started the procedure of establishing an IEP (Individualized Education Plan) that would allow Christine to receive academic accommodations moving into her high school years. Christine was assigned a case manager to work with her on the parameters of the IEP. Her case manager was another utterly amazing person who saw the real Christine and her potential. In the next few short months, Christine continued to grapple for control over her symptoms. These two women, the guidance counselor and the case manager, did nothing out of the ordinary. They merely said a few words of encouragement and spent a few minutes each day simply listening to Christine, but they positively impacted Christine's outlook on mental health awareness forever. It was then Christine started her advocacy to help all teenagers struggling with brain disorders or simply struggling with being a teenager.

Christine's mind is strong! Christine, like many other young people with brain disorders, has incredible intellect, perception, insight and understanding of people, surroundings, and interactions she experiences. She really does see and feel things that others cannot and most of those things are positive. Christine's intelligence and creativity allow her to connect to a large variety of people through her spoken word, her writing, and her music. Christine senses people in pain and comforts them. She senses true happiness in others and shares their joy. Christine has a finely-tuned sense of empathy for others that can bring incredible reassurance and well-being.

In the months that followed, Christine used her gifts to reach out to others who also struggled. She created a video explaining her diagnosis, her symptoms, and treatment so others could have a real life understanding of her challenge and reduce their fears. She made several gift packages for new teenage clients entering the Early Intervention Program filled with words of encouragement and actual coping tools, such as fidget toys. She joined the National Youth Board for the Psychosis Prevention Council to add a teenager's perspective to the committee. She became an intern for the International Bipolar Foundation and its *Say It Forward Campaign.*

Christine gave back by participating in interviews, motivational speaking, and performing concerts promoting not only how to survive with a mental challenge like bipolar disorder, but to gain strength from it. It is Christine's most sincere hope to change the way the world at large perceives mental illness by inviting every person who hears her voice—whether through this book, speaking appearances, music, social media, or her website—to join the Brain XP Community.

For the parents of a child with mental health challenges here are a few things I learned along the way:

Educate Yourselves. The most positive form of empowerment is knowledge. Read, read, read, and ask, ask, ask questions! There are a TON of information available and a TON of local resources. Get on the internet and find what's closest to you.

Be Observant. Why was Christine wearing a long sleeve sweatshirt in the middle of summer? Why did Christine stop watching our favorite game shows together after dinner? Why wouldn't Christine ever come out of her room? It could be your teen is just growing up and finding his or her own way, but don't be afraid to ask them. If something seems off, trust your instinct, something is likely off.

Stay Calm. If you are anything like me, you literally feel your child's pain as he or she is experiencing it and the pain may feel overwhelming to you as well as your child. Your child's empathy will make him or her feel the pain of both of you. This won't help them. The key to helping your child on this journey is being patient and remaining calm even when you feel distraught inside.

Take Care of Yourself. To nurture your ability to remain calm, you will need to take care of yourself. Force yourself to find time each day to pray, to relax, to read something inspirational—whatever gives you encouragement and internal strength. It will help you help your child.

Don't Lose Sight of Your Other Family Members. The nature of this journey is chaotic, but you will learn to navigate it over time. Your child will naturally be getting a lot of your time. Try to ensure no one gets lost in the shuffle. Encourage family meetings. Let everyone talk out any frustrations. Spend time together.

Forgive. This is a tough one—both my husband and I struggle with it to this day. Our child was hurt much more by the actions of others based on fear and stigma associated with her brain disorder than the illness itself. Perceptions take time to change. Don't waste your time in anger. Your child will need that time from you.

Start Small. Being a teenager in the 21st century is not easy. Your child does not need to be diagnosed with a brain disorder to benefit from a little help. I believe counseling is the most underutilized tool parents have available for their teenagers. Kids need to talk—and they don't always feel comfortable talking to their parents. There are all sorts of counseling services available at all different budget levels (including no budget). There are MANY teens out there struggling with short term bouts of depression and anxiety. A little counseling can teach them how to cope and empower them to make positive life choices.

Lastly, I learned the power of a few positive spoken words and the damage from a few negative spoken words. This is particularly burdensome for educators, coaches, and others in positions of authority with children. Over the last few years, we have been blessed to meet some of the most kind and generous people. After the pain of her removal from school, Christine received a hand-written note from the newly installed bishop in San Diego. The bishop committed to the mental health education of those working at the diocese and parishioners. Christine took enormous comfort in his message and still has his note posted on the wall of her bedroom. It was Christine's seventh-grade teacher's watchful eye that alerted us in the initial stages of her troubles. He was available to Christine any time she was willing to talk. His small acts of kindness allowed Christine to feel she was not alone. Every day Christine watched for her daily text from her friend who lived 2500 miles away and took much strength from knowing she was always in her corner. Every member of Christine's medical team provided support and encouragement. There was never a time they doubted her ability to take control of her symptoms and live the life she deserves. Christine took advantage of every positive word spoken to her when she decided to establish the Brain XP Community. Join Christine and become that positive word to the next teenager. Then, stand back and watch these amazing teenagers build our future.

A Friend's Perspective

Rachel XP

Christine and I have known each other ever since we were four years old. We attended the same school for six years. We were the best of friends. I remember on the first Friday of every month Christine, our brothers, and I would go to our local Round Table and stay there for hours playing games and eating pizza. We did that for years, until I changed schools at the start of sixth grade. However, I still lived in the same area as Christine and we would see each other occasionally. One of my favorite memories was going over to her house for her birthday one year after I had moved. She invited everyone from our class and we watched *The Outsiders*. Seeing her and my old friends again was amazing. We picked up like we had never been apart. I will never forget all of the memories we have made.

Soon after our get together, I learned that I would be moving to Tennessee. I remained close with Christine but eventually lost contact with my other friends. At first, I was upset, but soon I realized that Christine was my only true friend of that group. Even though I moved, and lived hundreds of miles away from her, we became closer. Shortly after moving, it became clear that I was also experiencing symptoms of mental illness. Knowing that Christine had coped with similar struggles, I told her about what I was going through and asked her for help. She gave me so much support and helped me through all of it! She was always there when I needed her, and I don't think I would have been able to overcome as many things as I did without her support, guidance, and encouragement.

Having this experience between the two of us brought us closer and we now understand each other even better. I am extremely proud of everything she has accomplished. Through her book, *Brain XP*, and all her recordings, Christine will continue to inspire, encourage, and educate many families and teens who struggle with mental illness and the not uncommon, but sometimes very difficult challenges of just being a teenager.

My Grandparents' Perspective

G-Ma XP and G-Pa XP

Christine

Through your darkest days it seems
You bring sunshine to those who dream.

Through your sadness and your fears
You bring joy to those who hear.

Through your confusion this is right
You bring to us understanding and light.

Through your mental problems dear
You made our understanding clear.

Through your music and your songs
You made right that which was wrong.

Through the heavy weight of your Cross
You have led many who were lost.

A cross that none of us could bear
You made the un-informed to care.

Grandparent Love

It is no wonder that we are so proud to have a granddaughter who cares so deeply, one who can share her pain and sorrows so that all humanity will be better served by her efforts to inform and to enlighten. Christine, your works will help ensure that others who suffer mental illnesses will not have to undergo the effects of rejection and misunderstanding.

Sometimes unspoken words are the cause of more injustice than words that are said aloud. For years ignorance existed because many words were unspoken concerning mental illness. When a young girl of twelve experienced the fright of unreal yet real voices and threats against those she loved, she was diagnosed with bipolar disorder. This young lady decided not to hibernate or lie down and feel sorry for herself, but to bring to light what had been hidden from the world for centuries. The illumination was simple: all mental illnesses are not the same and most who suffer mental illnesses are not violent or aggressive, but are very loving people. Only someone like Christine could reveal these things because, for this revelation to be discovered, it must have first been lived, experienced, and the Brain Expanded (XP). With a love for music and a talent for composing song lyrics, CHRISTINE MARIE FREY has revealed her experiences through and within her music and her book.

CHRISTINE XP

When we think of you little love
We think of angels far above
With lights so bright to pierce the night
And let us know everything's all right

These lines are for a girl named Christine
Whose life is filled with many dreams
Your music and your words we pray
Will bring you peace and joy today
And fill your heart with blessings and grace
Necessary for you and the human race

Now let us tell you of our love
As high as heaven is above
As deep as any ocean floor
And it reaches to the farthest shore

Now if this poem is bursting out
And in your heart you hear our shouts
We're proud of you each and everyday
And we love you in a gazillion ways
So may this day be ever blessed
By God in all His Holiness

About the Author

Christine is a 16-year-old teenager who lives in San Diego, California with her parents, Hans and Debbie, and older brother, James. Christine was brought up in a practicing Catholic family and went to private school from preschool to 8th grade. Christine  started having signs of depression and psychosis at age twelve. She received enormous support from her 7th grade teachers and school administration. She also started professional counseling when she was in the 7th grade. After struggling with self-harm, hallucinations, hospitalization, and her forced removal from school six months shy of her 8th grade graduation, Christine felt isolated and alone, but she never lost faith in God, her family, or herself. On her journey to wellness, Christine started journaling, writing song lyrics and music, and taught herself to play guitar as her primary coping strategies. Christine is dedicated to ending the stigma toward all teenagers with mental illness through Brain XP education. Christine's unique book describes her own real-life experiences as a young teenager suffering with mental illness. She uses the book, *Brain XP*, her contemporary music, videos, blog, social media, and public speaking to reach out to teenagers with mental illness. Christine shows them they are neither crazy nor alone. Rather, their brains are simply EXPANDED and they are unique!

Christine XP's Frequency

Sharing with teens across the world with mental illness.

You're not crazy and you're not alone.

You are Brain XP!

Visit

www.brainxpproject.com

and follow Christine's blog.

From Christine's Blog

December 13, 2017

I use the term mental illness in every day
conversation, but that's mainly because
it is understood. People have heard of it
and know what it means. I guess what
I struggle with is how people interpret
mental illness. Do they truly know what
it means?

Christine XP

From Christine's Blog

February 13, 2018

I researched for months trying to find reading material from a teenager like me, who could explain how they managed and coped in everyday life. I tried finding videos on YouTube and mental health related music from a teenager like me with messages that I could hear and feel less crazy. Sadly, I could not find anything that fit for me.

Christine XP

Brain XP

A resource for teenagers

www.brainxpproject.com

From Christine's Blog

February 20, 2018

I can acknowledge that I am a child of
God who deserves respect from everyone
which includes myself...I wrote a song
about it. It's called "Beautifull" of Love.
We are beautiful and we are all full of
love.

Christine XP

From Christine's Blog

February 26, 2018

#FEAR

Living in fear feels horrible. It breaks down your walls and puts you in a vulnerable position. Your guard is no longer existent, which exposes you to greater possibilities of getting hurt (emotionally and physically). I experienced this quite frequently as I worked through my psychotic symptoms.

Christine XP

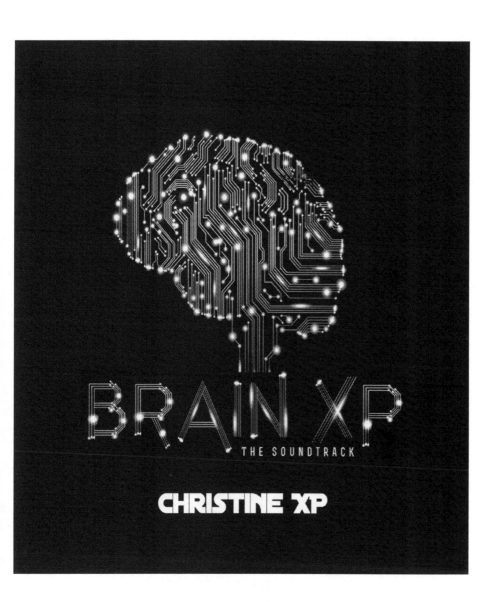

The Album

Online Mental Health Resources for Teens

www.nami.org/Find-Support/Teens-and-Young-Adults

www.nami.org/Get-Involved/NAMI-on-Campus

www.suicidepreventionlifeline.org

www.ok2talk.org

www.activeminds.org

www.strong365.org

www.bestbuddies.org

www.mindingyourmind.org/what-we-do/mental-health-education-program/in-school-clubs

www.bringchange2mind.org/get-involved/high-school-program

www.adolescenthealth.org

www.nimh.nih.gov/health/topics/child-and-adolescent-mental-health/index.shtml

www.mentalhealth.gov/talk/young-people

www.jedfoundation.org

www.mentalhealthamerica.net/back-school

www.teenmentalhealth.org

www.teenhealthandwellness.com/static/hotlines

www.yth.org/resources/mental-health/

www.hhs.gov/ash/oah

Made in the USA
Lexington, KY
15 November 2019

57117772R00094